UNCAGED

Trauma Recovery Using Facet Integration Technique

SPARROW SPAULDING

For Joey

CONTENTS

INTRODUCTION

Dear Precious Reader,

At last. I wish I had been ready to offer this book sooner, but the truth is I was still pulling out some deep roots which were obscuring the clarity needed to bring you an epic work on how to do what I have been doing my *entire* life: HEAL FROM TRAUMA.

On my quest for wholeness, I have come across dozens of works that have helped me to some degree, but each one was incomplete. Each time I threw myself into them, I emerged knowing there was still more. *My God*, has there been more.

I have spent decades working on myself and helping others heal from some of the most horrific abuses on the planet. The old adage is correct: You can only take your clients as far as you yourself have gone. I never stopped working to uncover all the ways trauma robs us of peace, joy, love, and self-worth. In the beginning, I did it more for my clients, but along the way I learned to love myself just as much. I declared that I deserved a beautiful life and committed to stopping at nothing to get there.

I turn 50 this year. I have spent nearly half a century trying to recover from all I have endured. This is the year I was finally able to pull out the deepest roots and my first instinct was to share with the world how to do what I have done.

This will not be a book filled with statistics on trauma and what a traumatized brain looks like on an MRI. There are plenty of books out there with that information and they are of value. This book is the how-to I wish I had. This is a collection of nearly everything I have done on my healing journey along with my own trauma recovery model I call Facet Integration Technique. This theory and technique have come from my years of observation, contemplation, and experimentation. I am over the moon to share it with you.

To get the most out of this book you must complete every exercise. Though you may have an inspiration or two if you are listening to this whilst running at the gym, you will not get the full healing experience. Many say they want to heal, yet they just stick a toe in. In order to heal, we need to swan dive into this work and show up for ourselves in a way we have never done before.

Are you ready? Only you can decide. Facing trauma takes courage, patience, dedication, and consistency. It takes showing up for yourself even when things get hard. If you have finally had enough, if you are READY for real healing, turn the page and let's get started...

MY STORY

Before we dive in, I want to take a moment and give you some background on my trauma roots. In case you didn't read my memoir, *Riding Standing Up*, here are the Cliff Notes.

I was kidnapped violently away from my mother at age three. I watched my mother get shoved across the parking lot of Dunkin' Donuts as my father came up from behind and grabbed me, throwing me into a car and driving away. My last vision of my mother was her lying on the ground, screaming for me. I didn't see her again for over a year.

I was taken across the country to live with my father's relatives. It was a messy, chaotic home with a vicious dog, and I lived in a near constant state of anxiety. I missed my mother dearly and thoughts of her are what kept me going. I slept with my cousin who wet the bed every night and soaked me. No one cleaned me up.

When I was returned to my mother, she was not the same. Having her children taken away was the beginning of her descent into mental illness. She frequently dissociated and wasn't at all interested in me. She didn't clean, barely cooked, and for years we grew up in poverty, often getting the lights cut off.

She had remarried her high school sweetheart, who had come back from Vietnam addicted to drugs and alcohol. He was a kind stepfather, but he drank away all our money and would frequently pass out. Nothing would wake him. He drank to quell the terrible PTSD he returned home with, and at times he would jump off the couch screaming, thinking he was still on the battlefield.

As the oldest, I grew up taking care of my younger siblings often. My mother divorced again and remarried when I was 11. She married a complete 'rageaholic' who had no love for my siblings and me and who became the quintessential drill sergeant in our lives. When he whisked my mother away to Nevada to get married, he left his 25-year-old brother in charge of my stepsister and myself. This man attempted to molest me, and I literally ran out of the house to save myself. I called my mother's best friend who didn't believe me. When my mother returned, she told me we would keep it quiet, so it didn't ruin her new marriage. A few months later, I went to the pediatrician for my 7th grade physical and my doctor sexually assaulted me during my visit. Once again, I told my mother, and she did nothing.

My teenage years were filled with drama. My stepfather started leering at me, and I knew I wasn't safe. Each night before bed I moved a heavy dresser in front of my bedroom door so no one could sneak in (it had happened in the past). My stepfather raged frequently, and I was sexually assaulted again two more times by dates in high school. Luckily, each time I was able to escape before it went too far.

Once I graduated and moved away, my mother went downhill fast. I spent most of my 20s dealing with my mother's mental illness and trying to get her help. She became schizophrenic and was horrible to deal with. I also had to sue to get guardianship of my youngest sister and eventually had to put my mother away. This took years and drained me physically, emotionally, and financially.

My adult relationships were often disasters because I had no idea how to choose the right partner. I only seemed to attract shelter pets, men in need, or complete narcissists. This is where the adult trauma started happening. Things like catching your husband with another man, remarrying a man with Bipolar and a sex addiction, and the best-finding out you are in a relationship with your stalker. I can't tell you the terror I felt finding out I had chosen someone who stalked me for months prior to meeting and hired a private investigator to find out every detail of my life. He came across me on the internet and somehow became obsessed. He infiltrated my organizations and made himself look like a true knight and I fell for it.

Throughout my adult years, I still managed to put myself through school, and have a career in helping others, all the while helping myself. I became dedicated to being the person I never had growing up.

I have spent the last 20 plus years in the trenches every day helping pull people out of the pit. I've learned a few things along the way, and now it's time to share my insights with the world. My goal is to get this out to as many people as possible because it's time to start healing. Limping through life just doesn't cut it.

It is my goal that this book will be the ultimate wake-up call. Lots of people do not have access to quality mental health assistance and while this book cannot take the place of that, it can cut right to the chase. If you take these exercises seriously, you can be on your way to living your best life. This book is an archaeological dig into YOU. If we truly want to heal (I prefer to say integrate) trauma, then we must go to the source.

There are many techniques out there that attempt to mask trauma, or bypass it by dealing with the vagus nerve, but going back in time is the gold standard. The trick is, we can't stay there forever, and we must not get lost in the weeds. This is time travel. We visit, get what we need, and then bring each part of us to present time. I'm going to take you back through this process step-by-step. If at any point during the work you become severely depressed, anxious, or even suicidal PLEASE reach out for help. Sometimes going back in time can be debilitating. I promise you it is still worth it, but you may need an experienced professional to help light your path and hold your hand. I have been so grateful for every therapist and life coach that has helped me on my journey. I have never been ashamed to ask for help and you should not be either. We are all humans, and we all do the best we can. But you're reading this book because you want *more*. More peace. More joy. More security. More adventure! And most importantly, you want you. **All of you.**

Buckle in. This is going to be one fantastic voyage!

 Sparrow

C H A P T E R

WHAT IS TRAUMA?

WHAT IS TRAUMA? THERE ARE LOTS OF DEFINITIONS CIRCULATING around as to the meaning of trauma. Also, there are different types of trauma. There is physical trauma, mental trauma, emotional trauma, spiritual trauma, and so forth. Much of trauma overlaps. Example: A man gets into a car accident and loses his leg. He experiences the physical trauma of pain and of not being able to walk. He has mental trauma from reliving the crash in his head (commonly called PTSD), he has emotional trauma from being devastated that he lost his leg, and he has spiritual trauma when his pastor visits him in the hospital and told him it was God's will that he lost his limb. Add onto this a loss of wages from work and a girlfriend that leaves him and where do we even start?

This is a drastic example to illustrate the different types of trauma we experience. What's important to note is that not all traumas are this gruesome. According to Oxford, trauma is "a deeply distressing or disturbing experience." This means that when you were in kindergarten and your babysitter accidentally dropped you off at the wrong class and you didn't recognize the teacher or the other students and you couldn't articulate that to anyone, you experienced trauma. This could happen to another kiddo who would not be fazed and would tell the teacher they were in the wrong class, but in your experience (being a bit shy) you cried and panicked and felt lost. It was *traumatizing*.

To our bodies, minds, and souls, trauma is trauma. Yes, there is a trauma continuum, but many factors contribute, especially age. The younger we are when we experience a trauma, the more it will impact us. What if I told you that the woman who was dropped off at the wrong Kindergarten became a level 5 control freak in her life to make sure that she always felt safe? She grew up in a stable home with parents who loved her, and life was rather "normal," but her early experience shaped how she saw the world, which was unsafe.

I could turn this whole book into a definition on trauma, but that would defeat the purpose. Instead, I will list out some common traumas, so you get the gist. Circle the ones that apply to you.

Physical Trauma- any intense physical pain or injury (intentional or unintentional), intense spanking, hitting, slapping, punching, kicking, excess yelling, hair-pulling, being yanked/jerked, being thrown up against a wall, biting, chokeholds, being robbed, having things thrown at you...you get the picture. It doesn't matter if it only happened one time if you were traumatized by it. Once is all it takes.

Sexual Trauma- unwanted/inappropriate touching, groping, penetration of any kind, someone exposing their genitalia, someone forcing you to expose yourself, inappropriate kissing, inappropriate comments, being shown pornography, being made to touch genitalia, rape, sodomy, being given an STI, becoming pregnant from a sexual assault, and more.

Mental/Emotional Trauma- being teased, being bullied, being manipulated, loud yelling, name-calling, chronic put-downs, emotional blackmail, gaslighting, raging, throwing objects, stonewalling, passive-aggressive behavior, cheating/emotional affairs with others, banging on doors when they're locked, alcohol abuse, living in poverty, witnessing inappropriate behavior from authority figures, living in squalor, and so on.

Spiritual Trauma- being told bad things that happen are your fault, God's will, etc. Being told too soon that "everything happens for a reason" and that your tragedy is a blessing in disguise. Being told by the church to stay in a very unhappy/abusive relationship, being abused by a church member, finding out your pastor uses drugs and sees male escorts when he preaches about the sins of homosexuality (think Pastor Ted Haggard), being raised in a strict religious environment where there is excess focus on hell and brimstone, having religious-addicted parents, being told you must have sex with a member of a church or religious cult because it's God's will, being groped by a pastor in recovery for sex addiction (that last one happened to me).

Cultural/Tribal/Racial Trauma-being told you are inferior because of your ethnicity or the color of your skin. Being told to hate another race or people because they are different from you. Having trauma passed down to you from ancestors (war, slavery, holocaust, and so on), being made to feel like you cannot be friends with or marry someone from a different race, being told you are acting like someone from another race, being ostracized because you are too light or too dark, being bullied because you do not follow your culture's political party lines, being shamed by your family for not living life according to cultural norms, and more.

How many of these did you circle? More than you were expecting? (Keep in mind this is a very incomplete list that only scratches the surface). Many of us have experienced these things and brush it off as "part of life." It's true, they can be a part of life. What's also true is that they will often fester inside of us and help determine who we become. We can brush off the intense pain of stubbing our toe even though it hurts like hell because we know it will heal eventually and there's usually no emotional experience attached to it. It's much harder to brush off when our father tells us we will amount to nothing, or our mother gets drunk and cuts our hair off in our sleep. Those are the traumas that stick.

List out your specific traumas here:

_____

_____

_____

_____

_____

_____

_____

_____

_____

_____

_____

_____

_____

_____

_____

_____

Many people are trauma survivors and don't even know it. I can't tell you how many clients I've had over the years that tell me they cannot remember their childhoods. A few years back I had a good friend recall being sexually abused at age five when she was 44 years old. It took THAT long for her memory to surface.

Even if you cannot remember a specific trauma, there are clues that can help determine if you could be an early trauma survivor. Check the ones that apply to you.

UNRESOLVED TRAUMA CHECKLIST

- ☐ Having chronic anxiety (mild, moderate, or severe) or panic attacks
- ☐ Not feeling comfortable in your own skin
- ☐ Being triggered by unexplained things or events (detesting the color purple, for example or hating a certain smell)
- ☐ Trouble sleeping, often with intense or scary dreams
- ☐ Fear of abandonment
- ☐ Continuously finding yourself in unhealthy relationships
- ☐ Substance abuse or dependence (including smoking)
- ☐ Addiction (food, television, social media, shopping, gambling, porn)
- ☐ Frequent need to check out
- ☐ Inherent need to stay busy
- ☐ Unexplained depression or dysthymia
- ☐ Finding yourself consistently in survival mode
- ☐ Procrastination
- ☐ Anger management issues (or being labeled a hair trigger)
- ☐ Fear of confrontation or conflict
- ☐ "Knowing" something happened to you at a certain age but not knowing what
- ☐ Emotional dysregulation

- ☐ Irrational fears or hypochondriasis
- ☐ Being embarrassed easily
- ☐ Social anxiety
- ☐ Feelings of shame
- ☐ Not being able to manage money properly
- ☐ Inability to feel emotions (good or bad) or "numbness"
- ☐ Having good intuition and being able to "sense" danger or a bad person
- ☐ Any kind of self-mutilation (can include multiple piercings or tattoos)
- ☐ Constantly worrying about what others think
- ☐ Being different in public versus at home
- ☐ Not wanting to participate in life outside of the requirements
- ☐ Not trusting others
- ☐ Not having friends
- ☐ Constantly finding things to complain about
- ☐ Brain fog and lack of focus
- ☐ Perfectionism
- ☐ Frequent physical pains or ailments (or disease)
- ☐ Avoids sex or being touched (including hugs)
- ☐ Overreacts to minor frustrations
- ☐ Black and white thinking
- ☐ Feeling like the world is not in your favor
- ☐ Being overly preoccupied with sex
- ☐ Having lots of clutter or hoarding tendencies
- ☐ Acting like life is always wonderful. "No bad days"
- ☐ Talking too much or not enough
- ☐ Fear of being alone
- ☐ Unstable relationships

This is by no means an exhaustive list, but it's a great start. How many did you check? If you checked one or two, that doesn't necessarily mean you have unacknowledged trauma in your past. If you checked more than a few, it's a question worth exploring. Since you're reading this book, you probably have a good idea that you experienced trauma at some point in your life, but you may have a friend or family member who is still in the dark. Give them this checklist and see if any lights go off.

CHAPTER

TIME TRAVEL 101

RECENTLY, A FRIEND TOLD ME HE DIDN'T THINK WE EVER *FULLY* RE-cover from childhood trauma, and I agree. At first, this left me dis-heartened. The more I thought about it, the more I realized I don't want to fully recover from trauma. Yes, you read that right. If I fully recovered, it would be like the trauma never happened. But the reality is it *did* happen, and I am forever changed because of it. The quest then becomes how do I turn the experience into a superpower? This is the work of trauma integration.

I think it's desperately difficult, exhausting, and arduous, but I do believe it's possible. I don't think it happens overnight. It certainly didn't for me. Trauma integration happens in stages and is a hero's journey. For much of my life I have felt like Link in the Legend of Zelda, on an intense odyssey to collect the eight fragments of the "Triforce Wisdom" and gain access to the royal princess. Only I feel like I have been blindfolded through much of the journey and not knowing where I will find any of the necessary fragments, AND I keep stubbing my toe along the way. But the pull has been strong, because even though

I am Link I am also Princess Zelda, on a quest to save myself. It is the only way.

I am guessing that most of you reading this book are survivors of early childhood trauma. If you weren't, you could easily read a Tony Robbins book or something by Eckhart Tolle and happily be on your path to peace and prosperity. I'm also guessing that you may have already read those authors, or other books by people like Brené Brown, Brendon Burchard, and whoever else is on Oprah's recommended list. Yet something is still missing. You're *still* stuck.

When I began my healing, it felt like I was starting in the middle, though I couldn't articulate that at the time. I learned some important things about myself, but it was like putting together a jigsaw puzzle without all of the pieces. There were holes, and I was attempting to fill those holes with anything that seemed to fit. It wasn't until I wrote a memoir of my childhood that I saw the value in going back in time and scrutinizing the important moments. I was surprised no therapist had ever asked me to do it. I had therapists that touched on some of the early events but never in a way that connected all the dots. I needed to retell the story of me and how I became the person I am today. Now it's your turn.

EXERCISE #2

List out the 10 most impactful moments in your life, good or bad. Go as far back as you can.

1.

2.

3.

4.

5.

6.

7.

8.

9.

10.

How do you feel looking at this list? Was it easy or hard to complete? What patterns and themes do you notice, if any?

_____

_____

_____

_____

_____

_____

_____

_____

_____

_____

Now you're ready for the next step.

EXERCISE #3

Write a bio. I want you to include as much information as possible and start as early as you can. What was going on in your parents' lives when you mother was carrying you? What was happening in the world at that time (i.e. did Kennedy just get shot?) What was your mom's labor and delivery like? If you're a woman was your father disappointed that you weren't a boy? Try and get as much of this information as you can. If you do not have access to it just start where you are able.

How were you as a toddler? Shy? Outgoing? How did your parents raise you? Were there any alcoholics in the home? Was there any abuse taking place? What was school like? Did you have separation anxiety? Did you wet your pants in kindergarten? Try and leave no stone un-turned during this process. It's often the little events that are the keys to great insight.

Did you like your classmates? Your teachers? What was your school identity like? Did you experience divorce at any time in your development? Did anyone pass away (parents, grandparents, siblings, pets, other family)? Did you watch your dad accidentally run the family dog over with the car?

Talk about how junior and senior high school were like. Did you get teased or bullied? Were you part of the clique or left out? How did you see yourself during those tough years? Did you feel awkward? What kind of student were you? Did anyone sit you down and talk about your future? Did you father a child or get pregnant in high school? Did you get hit on by a teacher? Go there…

After high school continue writing and make a timeline of major events. First job, college, having children, buying a home, losing a loved one, etc. Did you get in trouble with the law? When did you start drinking or smoking cigarettes if applicable? Did your relationship with your parents change? Who was your first big heartbreak? Think back…

Lastly, I want you to bring yourself up to present time. What do you struggle with in life? Are relationships an issue? Excess weight? Low self-esteem? Are you constantly struggling financially? Do you have problems with focus and concentration? Energy? Is your health starting to take a dive? Are you battling major illness? Are your kids having problems? Do you struggle with parenting? Do you drink too much? Are you on several antidepressants that aren't working well? Again, leave no stone unturned in this process. We are going to connect some fascinating dots!

> *The longest bio I have ever received from a client was 17 pages, single spaced. If you can write one that long, Bravo! I would say try and write no less than five pages, otherwise your bio may be incomplete. I would get a journal or notebook for this exercise. Give yourself at least several days to a week to complete it but try not to take longer than that. Otherwise, you may lose steam.

What was this experience like? What patterns and themes did you uncover?

_____

_____

_____

_____

_____

_____

What did you discover about yourself that you didn't realize before?

_____

_____

_____

_____

How are you like your mother or father?

_____

_____

_____

_____

Many say writing a bio is nerve-wracking and can kick up some negative emotions. How did you feel writing it?

_____

_____

_____

_____

Most of my clients enjoy the process overall as they start to see patterns even before we begin discussing it. Very few people take the time to dig this much into their past but remember-hidden gems are buried. We have to mine them. And you, my friend, are a diamond. A diamond with many facets.

CHAPTER

DISCOVERING YOUR FACETS

"The real self is not I, but we."

-*FRITZ KUNKEL*

I USED TO LOVE THE SONG, "COAT OF MANY COLORS" BY DOLLY PARTON. I grew up poor, and I thought if she could make something of herself with such humble beginnings there was no stopping me. At some point during my trauma recovery work, I thought of her patchwork coat, and it reminded me of the many different "colors" inside of each one of us. As I continued to research and work toward healing it occurred to me that I didn't have to use the analogy of an unsightly pieced-together garment to understand myself. Instead, I could envision a diamond. After all, diamonds are hard, beautiful, and shiny. They sparkle. The more facets they have, the more they shine and reflect light.

I knew I was a diamond, but have you ever seen a diamond before it is cut and polished? It looks like a dirty, cloudy rock. A true "diamond in the rough." That was me, and that's probably you, too. Guess what? Now, it's time to shine! Let's start polishing those facets so we can see the TRUE gem you are.

THE FACETS OF ME PART 1

Most of us go through life and never realize that there are different aspects of our selves that live within us. We've all heard of the "inner child," but it's a vague concept that doesn't bring much self-awareness. This exercise is designed to help you get to know yourself on a very intimate level which helps us heal trauma, integrate, and learn to love ourselves in a profound way. When we experience early trauma, parts of us get frozen in time. This is why you have the intention of staying away from sweets and find yourself eating them again and again. It's not necessarily a lack of will power. It often is a younger "facet" of you that is addicted to sugar and medicates her feelings by indulging.

We have all heard of "Sybil" and the concept of Multiple Personality Disorder. It is rare but does exist and is often the result of absolute horrific trauma occurring early in life. Most likely no one reading this book is struggling with MPD (now called Dissociative Identity Disorder). DID and Facets are not one and the same, though the concept is similar. In my experience we *all* have facets, even if we had the most stable of childhoods.

Complete this exercise in a quiet place free of distractions. If you have a houseful of kids and pets go to the library or a local coffee shop. Sit with yourself and close your eyes to focus on each facet of you. When you think of your earliest facet, how old is he/she? What is she wearing? Is she smiling? Crying? Go into it, almost as if you are immersing your-self into a good book or movie. If you find more than the ones listed here, please describe. Try and be as detailed as possible when filling out each section. If you have difficulty remembering (esp. with the very young self) try asking a family member for help.

My Very Young Self (3-5ish)

Approx Age: _____ Name: _____

Traits and Characteristics:

_____
_____
_____
_____
_____
_____
_____
_____
_____
_____
_____

My triggers (then and now):

_____
_____
_____
_____
_____
_____

How I am useful/protective (then and now):

_____

_____

_____

_____

_____

_____

_____

_____

_____

How I can be self-defeating (then and now):

_____

_____

_____

_____

_____

_____

_____

_____

_____

What are my needs?

_____

_____

_____

_____

_____

_____

What's my biggest fear?

_____

_____

_____

_____

_____

_____

What are the false narratives I have created?

_____

_____

_____

_____

_____

_____

My Preadolescent Self (Grade School)

Approx Age: _____   Name: _____

Traits and Characteristics:

_____

_____

_____

_____

_____

_____

_____

_____

_____

_____

_____

My triggers (then and now):

_____

_____

_____

_____

_____

_____

How I am useful/protective (then and now):

_____

_____

_____

_____

_____

_____

_____

_____

_____

How I can be self-defeating (then and now):

_____

_____

_____

_____

_____

_____

_____

_____

_____

What are my needs?

_____

_____

_____

_____

_____

_____

What's my biggest fear?

_____

_____

_____

_____

_____

_____

What are the false narratives I have created?

_____

_____

_____

_____

_____

My Adolescent Self (Jr High)

Approx Age: _____ Name: _____

Traits and Characteristics:

_____
_____
_____
_____
_____
_____
_____
_____
_____
_____
_____

My triggers (then and now):

_____
_____
_____
_____
_____
_____

How I am useful/protective (then and now):

_____

_____

_____

_____

_____

_____

_____

_____

_____

How I can be self-defeating (then and now):

_____

_____

_____

_____

_____

_____

_____

_____

_____

What are my needs?

_____

_____

_____

_____

_____

What's my biggest fear?

_____

_____

_____

_____

_____

What are the false narratives I have created?

_____

_____

_____

_____

_____

My Late Adolescent Self (High School)

Approx Age: _____   Name: _____

Traits and Characteristics:

_____

_____

_____

_____

_____

_____

_____

_____

_____

_____

My triggers (then and now):

_____

_____

_____

_____

_____

_____

How I am useful/protective (then and now):

_____

_____

_____

_____

_____

_____

_____

_____

_____

How I can be self-defeating (then and now):

_____

_____

_____

_____

_____

_____

_____

_____

_____

What are my needs?

_____

_____

_____

_____

_____

_____

What's my biggest fear?

_____

_____

_____

_____

_____

_____

What are the false narratives I have created?

_____

_____

_____

_____

_____

_____

My Early Adult Self

Approx Age: _____   Name: _____

Traits and Characteristics:

_____

_____

_____

_____

_____

_____

_____

_____

_____

_____

_____

My triggers (then and now):

_____

_____

_____

_____

_____

_____

How I am useful/protective (then and now):

_____

_____

_____

_____

_____

_____

_____

_____

_____

How I can be self-defeating (then and now):

_____

_____

_____

_____

_____

_____

_____

_____

_____

What are my needs?

_____

_____

_____

_____

_____

What's my biggest fear?

_____

_____

_____

_____

_____

What are the false narratives I have created?

_____

_____

_____

_____

_____

Below is an example of my own Facet work to help give you inspiration. Notice how I use "I" and "she" interchangeably. She IS me and yet she is also a distinct part of me and so it feels appropriate to use both.

My Very Young Self:

Little Sparrow

Age 3

Traits: She's excited about life. Loves her mom and grandma. Loves books. Picky eater. Loves her dogs. Loves Sesame Street and her Katie doll. Loves her room and riding her tricycle through the house. Loves her gingerbread lip balm pin from Avon. Loves chocolate donut holes. Is scared of vampires because her grandma watches Dark Shadows when she babysits. Loves her friend Kimmy from next door. Did not like being away from her mom. Loves her grandpa.

Triggers: Being abducted by Dad. She was traumatized. She saw her mother on the ground, screaming. Felt alone. She had nothing when she was taken-no clothes, no toys, no books. She lost her excitement for life and missed her mother dearly. She didn't like her uncle's messy home and was afraid of his mean, growling dog. Didn't like taking naps. She became intimidated and lost her self-esteem. Being peed on by her cousin made her feel powerless. (Still get triggered by the smell of urine). Felt worthless when Dad wouldn't clean me up. Became numb. Also became a caregiver to my younger brother during this time, and other people trying to care for him would trigger me since I thought it was my job. Today, lying and betrayal are still huge triggers for me most likely due to being abducted. Besides being traumatized, I was completely broken-hearted. I was so in love with my mother and being ripped away from her felt like death. Devastated doesn't even cover it. Today, when I really care about someone (like a significant other) I go through a phase where I am afraid they will die on me. I make sure we have good life insurance so I'm never "left with nothing" again.

How I am useful? She's the joyful one. Loves learning and loves life. Loves reading, animals, and her family. She also holds the sadness and trauma of the abduction. She's independent and mature. She doesn't let heartbreak annihilate her. She's strong.

How I am self-defeating? She used to let the sadness override any joy. Sometimes it's still hard to feel joy-she has to really focus on it. Numbness can take over quickly. She used to hide a lot before getting help. She also used to have meltdowns by herself to let the trauma out.

What are my needs? Safety, love, affection, attention, someone to engage with her and be a playmate. Chocolate donut holes (or some kind of chocolate treat), words of affirmation, tactile soothers like fuzzy socks and blankets. Her stuffed bear. **She needs to feel cherished.**

Biggest Fear: That she will never see Mom again. Now: That she will never feel cherished again.

False Narrative: It takes another person to make me feel cherished.

My Preadolescent Self

Approx. Age 8-11

Name: "Puppy"

Traits: Loves Snoopy, hates bathing, always playing outside, defiant to Mom, wants things her way, hates school, likes her room clean, loves her electric blue carpet, loves junk food, loves bubblegum, is the ringleader of the neighborhood, loves all animals (including reptiles), loves stickers, painfully shy at school, doesn't like her teachers, doesn't want structure and feels happiest when there are no rules, loves to read, advanced intellectually, loves her EZ bake oven, Speak and Spell™, and Strawberry Shortcake™ dolls, wants to be left alone so she can enjoy life, likes clothes, purses, and accessories like jewelry.

Triggers: Mom's smoking, Stepdad Frank's drinking, being poor and not being able to pay bills, getting electricity cut off. Mom kicking Frank out made me wall my heart off even more and started losing respect for authority, including teachers. Started feeling self-conscious for being poor and smelling like cigarette smoke. Started eating junk food to feel better since it was a quick, cheap thrill. Was triggered when people didn't listen to me and told me what to do. When snow got into the holes in my shoes. Now: I can't stand running out of things. I get anxiety when a large bill comes in even though I have plenty of funds to pay it.

How I am useful: She puts her needs first. She sees through other people's bullshit. She's a leader. She's smart, imaginative, and knows how to get her way. She doesn't like drama. She's direct and to the point. She stands up for herself.

How I can be self-defeating: She's stubborn, likes too many things her own way, can pester and not let things drop. She doesn't like routine like washing her face at night. She procrastinates and can ignore problems. She can ice someone out after a few letdowns (like she had to do with Frank) and can ignore other people's needs.

What are her needs? She needs one makeup free day a week. Alone time, freedom, a stocked fridge, and pantry, play time, reading time, outdoor activities, safety, and security. She'd like to be able to rely on the adults in her life (these days) but also needs to rely on herself. She likes to be put together and likes her teeth white. **Core need:** She needs to be able to enjoy life while having structure.

Biggest fear: She's afraid that stupid adults will ruin her life.

False narrative: Total freedom is the answer.

Junior High Self

Name: Sparrow

Age: 11

Traits: Optimistic, mature, likes to sing into her hairbrush and create dance routines, loves Michael Jackson and the Thriller album, loves the Go Gos, had a great experience in 6th grade with classmates and teacher and now loves school, likes seeing her mother more stable (after moving in with stepdad #2), starting to be more trusting. Loves to play pranks. Loves being left-handed and wearing her lacy "Madonna" glove on her left hand.

Triggers: My step-uncle attempting to molest me and no one believing me. Mom then brushing it under the carpet to avoid "ruining her new marriage," starting 7th grade and feeling like a very small fish in a big pond, mean teachers, being sexually abused by my pediatrician during my 7th grade physical and now feeling like I couldn't trust any adults in my life. Seeing how my stepfather had no patience for my little brother, and later for me. Stepfather's rageful screaming and constant punishment.

How she is useful: She is the one that is musical- likes to sing and play the piano, has great taste in music, loves learning, likes to put outfits together.

How she is self-defeating: She doesn't trust anyone, closes up easily, feels like she has to step in and continue being a parent to her little brother and protect him, loses hope easily.

What are her needs? She needs safety and protection from adults. She needs to feel heard and believed. She needs to feel valued. She needs to be a kid and leave the parenting to the adults. **Core need:** She needs to keep the faith.

What is her biggest fear? That all adults are unsafe and will eventually annihilate her.

False narrative: Everyone has an ulterior motive.

My Adolescent Self

Age 14-16

Name: Sparrow

Traits: Sarcastic, brooding, dry, sometimes naughty sense of humor, loves fashion, loves her maternal grandparents, mothers her younger siblings, felt awkward looks wise until age 15, enjoys attention from boys, wants to grow up badly, likes to smoke, likes to drink occasionally, doesn't feel like she fits in at school, shy except with close friends, wishes she was French, loves wearing makeup, annoyed by her little brother, spends a lot of time alone in her room, intuitive, feels pain deeply, wants to know the meaning of life and why she's here, can't wait to leave home, loves to write and journals daily, still loves to sing and dance, wishes someone would see her pain, loves to write songs, loves trying to solve mysteries, believes in ghosts, aliens, and past lives, hates having so many chores, likes getting money from her father, smokes when she has uncomfortable feelings, likes to occasionally check out with weed, can't stand Stepdad #2.

Triggers: Mom becoming more mental and checking out with medication disgusted me. Stopped doing homework and caring about school because I was also checking out. Realized how many perverts were out there and that also disgusted me, Stepdad being so authoritarian caused me to become rebellious and mouthy, hated being under his thumb, little brother drove me nuts, became soft in a way when I met my first love, then hard again when he moved away. Any kind of lying and betrayal still triggers me.

How am I useful? Great sense of style, quick wit, funny, deep thinker, sticks up for others, talented writer, great at taking care of kids, good ear for music, loves to research, good listener, insightful, independent thinker, good sister, good friend.

How am I self-defeating? Can be reclusive (esp when writing), can say some biting things, attracted to the wrong boys/men, can be shy, wants to be liked (then), too boy crazy (then), can be lazy (then), not health-conscious (then).

What are my needs? To be seen and valued, alone time, creative time, to feel attractive, meaning and purpose, friends who want to talk about deep things, guidance, and someone to talk to. She needs to know she's loved. She needs for her basic needs to be provided for. **Core need:** To truly love and see herself.

Biggest Fear: No one will ever see me and my true worth.

False narrative: People don't value me. I'm invisible.

My Late Adolescent/Early Adult Self:

Age: 17-20

Name: "Business" Sparrow

Traits: Responsible, level-headed, logical, go-getter, strong work ethic, a bit boring, always working, wants to get her life together, saves money, craves a drama-free existence, buried heartbreak about her past, wants to stop worrying about others so much, feels like she has to do everything on her own, becomes a caretaker to family from a distance (after she moves away for college).

Triggers: The thought of not having money, my mother's craziness, rude and disrespectful people, victim mentality, lazy people, messy people, when people watch too much television, play video games excessively, people who don't read or develop themselves. Dislikes useless arguing, people overindulging in their feelings, and loses respect when people fall apart.

How am I useful? Makes money, pays bills, gets things done, went to college three times, puts hard work into personal development like dance lessons, tennis lessons, foreign language, music lessons. Reads incessantly and is constantly learning. Loves to research. Makes plans for the future. Keeps a tight schedule. Detail-oriented and great leadership abilities.

How am I self-defeating? She works too much, lets herself become depleted, takes on too much, doesn't ask for help, keeps going like a machine. She shuts off her feelings so they don't get in the way of her accomplishments. She blocks her inability to feel pain or exhaustion. She takes on other people's problems so she doesn't have to feel the pain of sitting by and watching them flounder.

What are my needs? To rest, take breaks, appreciation for her hard work, consistent rewards, a vacation, naps, less responsibility, to let others fail. She is deep-down bone tired and could use a month on a desert island. She needs more fun and to be frivolous occasionally. She needs to laugh and have more joy.

Biggest fear: That I will be responsible for others until I die.

False narrative: Everyone needs me all the time.

ASSESSMENT

What did you learn about yourself from this exercise?

_____

_____

_____

_____

_____

_____

_____

_____

What I learned when I did this exercise is that when I got sad or depressed it was my early facet who awakened, since she held the sadness for all of me. This explains why during adolescence I would sometimes hide in a closet and cry for hours sometimes, clutching a stuffed animal, and often rocking back and forth. Each time I did this, I relived that devastation of being taken from my mother (though I didn't know that's what was happening at the time) and it would wreck me. I would have to sleep for hours and hours to even have enough energy to function the next day. I would only do this when no one was around, and as a result no one knew what I was going through, not that they would have understood, anyway. I'm sure people would have just thought that the very put-together Sparrow had lost her marbles.

I also learned that when I became rebellious and defiant it was my inner 8-year-old grade school self who learned not to trust authority figures. She wanted to be left alone to live life on her own terms. This meant junk food, no baths, no bedtime, and certainly no school. Even today she still tries to run the show at times. She shows up when I'm tired and tries to get me to go to bed without taking off my makeup. She also tries to get me to stay up late watching YouTube videos. Both she and my earliest facet band together and try to get me to eat gluten free chocolate donut holes, since Mom and I were on our way into Dunkin' Donuts™ to get Munchkins when Dad kidnapped me.

WHAT NOW?

Now that you have a good sense of your developmental facets, it's time to take the next step. This is where it becomes interesting. You get to parent these parts of you. That's right, just like you parent your own children (if you have them). These are all parts of you that need the two best things that parents offer: love and discipline (i.e., boundaries and instruction).

The first step in parenting is getting to know them. Study your facets work and commit as much to memory as possible. For instance, it's my job to know that little three-year-old Sparrow loves books, animals, being in nature, etc. and I need to make sure she gets a steady dose of those things. I need to spend time with her and *be* with her. To this day I have an 8x10 picture of her in my office right above my computer so I can see her throughout the day. He radiant smile reminds me that she is precious and that it's my job to love and care for her. Often, we want others to do the job, and will become disenchanted when our spouses don't pamper us or tell us how wonderful we are. While it's nice when others show up for us, nothing takes the place of showing up for yourself.

Showing up also means setting boundaries. There are many times I say no to the tasty yet calorie dense gluten free chocolate donut holes because sweets are not a big part of my meal plan. I do, however, negotiate with my little one. I often let her have some unsweetened chocolate almond milk with stevia, or a Sambazon™ Açai bite after dinner. It's a win-win. If I ignored her need for a sweet treat enough times, she might band with some of the other facets and send me to the bakery for German chocolate cupcakes and then I would be a goner! That's how much our facets control our thoughts and behavior. We will find ourselves saying or intending one thing only to repeatedly get off course and go in another direction, typically the direction that keeps us stuck in self-sabotage.

The other thing I want you to focus on is the false narrative for each developmental facet. When you find yourself irritated, sad, upset, or triggered, stop and ask yourself which facet is unhappy and what the false narrative is she is buying into at the moment. Overcoming a false narrative is like trying to turn a steering wheel with no power steering. It's tough at first, but is a critical part of trauma integration. A false narrative like, "Other people matter more than me" can truly ruin our lives if we continue to buy into it. When you uncover a false narrative **correct** it by stating the truth. "No one matters more than me" might be a nice correction or "I matter just as much as everyone else" is a truthful replacement. We are looking for truth and if we are committed to this work then we are committed to truth.

> **Note:**
> False narratives are lies. Lies are painful and cause suffering. Whenever we have a thought or feeling that feels bad it's a lie. We can always deal with the truth, even if it's hard. The pain of a lie is distinct and there's no peace in it. Pay attention and you will be able to discern between fact and fiction.

HERE'S HOW

Every morning before you start your day sit up straight with your eyes closed. I want you to get grounded in your body first and foremost. If you're sitting on the floor imagine you have roots like a tree growing out of your bottom and deep into the Earth. Breathe and pay attention to your breath. Sometimes, I imagine water getting poured on the top of my head and it comes down and fills up every square inch inside my body. Feel the weight of your arms and legs. Focus your attention to your chest. Is it tight? Focus on your mid-section. What are the sensations? This whole process only takes a minute or so. Take longer if you have the time.

When you feel rooted in your body, check in with each facet, starting with the youngest one. Ask her how she's doing and what she needs today. Does she need a walk in nature? Time with her pets? What do the others need? My 8-year-old needs alone time. My teenage self needs to feel creative and pretty, and my early adult needs to feel organized. I ask every day because often these needs change. Sometimes the adolescent needs to read, and sometimes my early adult needs rest.

It is *critical* not to skip this step. The more you work to parent these parts of you, the more they will feel safe and loved and the more control you will have over your thoughts, feelings, and emotions. When you do get an unhappy thought, you can ask yourself which part of you it is coming from. Then, you can check in with that part and see how you can help. It's very important to be the adult in our lives and not let these younger versions of us run the show. Otherwise, our lives and relationships will suffer. We will never get off the hamster wheel of trauma.

When you have successfully connected with your facets and have consistently been listening to and parenting them, it's time to go onto the next step. This is where it gets 'facet-nating'.

THE FACETS OF ME PART 2

Often, when we have experienced trauma, in addition to having facets that are stuck in time at various ages, we will have spinoff facets that develop to help us navigate through the world. These facets typically start developing at a certain age but can continue to develop over several years. You may find that some are more mature than others, but they may seem rather ageless, unlike the facets you discovered in part 1 of this exercise.

Take some time to think about your personality. Are you a go-getter? A worker bee? Do you have a temper when you get pushed? Do you have a side that likes to enjoy the finer things in life? Do you have a side that likes to mother and care for everyone? These are the spinoffs that evolved out of your developmental facets. We must get to know them and what makes them tick as part of the trauma recovery process. Some may seem fun, almost innocuous, while others may seem like demons. I promise you all these facets are valuable and have much to teach us. Learning about yourself on this level is a total gamechanger. When I did this work on myself, I found that I had an inner Queen Bee who loves office supplies, delegating tasks, getting things done, and writing in a planner. She keeps my business running smoothly. She can get out of hand if she starts delegating too many tasks to others or judging them if they aren't as organized as she is. Every day I check in with her to see what her needs are. On the surface, she will say she needs a clean desk, but what I really know about her is that she needs to avoid chaos and for things to run smoothly. She definitely doesn't like surprises!

It's important to name your spinoffs appropriately, so really think about this. Please don't choose any derogatory names, as we will learn *all* our facets have value. You may discover more than six. If so, use your journal or notebook to keep going! ☺

Facet Spinoff #1

Name: _____

Traits:

_____

_____

_____

_____

_____

_____

What age did he/she start developing and why?

_____

_____

_____

How is he/she useful?

_____

_____

_____

_____

_____

How is he/she self-defeating?

_____

_____

_____

_____

What are his/her needs? (Surface and core)

_____

_____

_____

_____

What is his/her biggest fear?

_____

_____

_____

_____

What is the false narrative he/she believes?

_____

_____

Facet Spinoff #2

Name: _____

Traits:

_____

_____

_____

_____

_____

_____

What age did he/she start developing and why?

_____

_____

_____

How is he/she useful?

_____

_____

_____

_____

_____

How is he/she self-defeating?

_____

_____

_____

_____

What are his/her needs? (Surface and core)

_____

_____

_____

_____

What is his/her biggest fear?

_____

_____

_____

_____

What is the false narrative he/she believes?

_____

_____

Facet Spinoff #3

Name: _____

Traits:

_____

_____

_____

_____

_____

_____

What age did he/she start developing and why?

_____

_____

_____

How is he/she useful?

_____

_____

_____

_____

_____

How is he/she self-defeating?

_____

_____

_____

_____

What are his/her needs? (Surface and core)

_____

_____

_____

_____

What is his/her biggest fear?

_____

_____

_____

_____

What is the false narrative he/she believes?

_____

_____

Facet Spinoff #4

Name: _____

Traits:

_____

_____

_____

_____

_____

_____

What age did he/she start developing and why?

_____

_____

_____

How is he/she useful?

_____

_____

_____

_____

_____

How is he/she self-defeating?

_____

_____

_____

_____

What are his/her needs? (Surface and core)

_____

_____

_____

_____

What is his/her biggest fear?

_____

_____

_____

_____

What is the false narrative he/she believes?

_____

_____

Facet Spinoff #5

Name: _____

Traits:
_____
_____
_____
_____
_____
_____

What age did he/she start developing and why?
_____
_____
_____

How is he/she useful?
_____
_____
_____
_____
_____

How is he/she self-defeating?

_____

_____

_____

_____

What are his/her needs? (Surface and core)

_____

_____

_____

_____

What is his/her biggest fear?

_____

_____

_____

_____

What is the false narrative he/she believes?

_____

_____

Facet Spinoff #6

Name: _____

Traits:

_____

_____

_____

_____

_____

_____

What age did he/she start developing and why?

_____

_____

_____

How is he/she useful?

_____

_____

_____

_____

_____

How is he/she self-defeating?

_____

_____

_____

_____

What are his/her needs? (Surface and core)

_____

_____

_____

_____

What is his/her biggest fear?

_____

_____

_____

_____

What is the false narrative he/she believes?

_____

_____

Below is an example of some of my spinoff facets. It's important to try to determine what triggered the spinoff to develop.

Facet Spinoff from: Preadolescent "Puppy"

Name: Miss Polly Purebread

Age she started developing: 8 Reason: Spending time with my dad and stepmother had a large influence on this facet spinoff. My stepmother was the queen of manners and presentation. Everything was always perfect on the surface. She would dress me in fancy clothing and put my hair in buns for pictures or special occasions. She had a lot of class and it made me feel safe even though I was intimidated by it.

Traits: Perfectionistic, proper, demure, principled, religious, likes classic 1940s clothing with pearls, against immoral behavior- things like pornography, gambling, and overindulgence of any kind. Has impeccable manners, likes her clothing to match. Doesn't like when her nails are chipped. Wishes she could wear white gloves when she leaves the house.

How she is useful: She keeps me out of trouble. Holds to her values. Tells the truth. Has great social skills and grace in public settings. Loves to have dinner parties and entertain. Sends birthday cards and thank-you notes.

How she is self-defeating: Can be judgmental of others. Drops friends if they don't have enough class or if they have poor manners. Gets easily disgusted with people. Worries too much about her weight and physical appearance, whether she has something in her teeth, or if she has a hair out of place. She can be overly conscientious and notices dust on her baseboards. Feels unsettled if her house looks lived in.

What are her needs: To remind herself that she doesn't have to be perfect to be loved or to matter. Needs to remember that others are not as conscientious as her. Needs to feel appreciated for her efforts. Needs time to beautify and be creative with fashion.

Core need: To approve of and appreciate herself.

Biggest fear: That no one (especially a man) will be good enough to respect.

False narrative: Everything must be perfect all the time or else it is unacceptable.

Facet Spinoff: Very Young Sparrow Age 3

Name: Fierce One

What age did she start developing? 3 Reason: Being abducted by my father and forced into hiding at my uncle's house for over a year. This was the most traumatizing experience of my life.

Traits: Protective, fearless, ruthless, mean, savage, morbid. Will really let someone have it if they cross the line. Likes John Wick movies. Can be very cutting with her words. Can be condescending as hell if someone deserves it. She's an expert at embarrassing someone if they rub her the wrong way (after being warned). Has no problem with people she doesn't care for dying. She feels relieved and secretly celebrates.

How she is useful: She will step in when necessary and protect herself and her family. She's not afraid to confront people or to say no. She can be intimidating when necessary. She has been able to fight her way out of several scary situations. She enforces boundaries. She has a great sixth sense for danger and is always aware of her surroundings and who is nearby. She refuses to be caught off guard.

How she is self-defeating: When she shows up, she can be overly aggressive because she feels like she has to do damage control, esp if her L'il Mama facet has let someone walk all over her. She's myopic and wants to solve things through intimidation, yelling, and insults, which can create drama.

What are her needs? She needs respect. She would also like to be appreciated. She'd like to feel safe and like she doesn't always have to come in and do the ass-kicking.

Core need: To respect herself.

Biggest fear: That she will go too far and get in trouble.

False Narrative: One must be feared to be respected.

Facet Spinoff: Very Young Sparrow Age 3

Name: L'il Mama

What age did she start developing? 3 Reason: When I was abducted at age 3, I was reunited with my brother who was taken before me. He was barely a year old, and I felt like it was my job to step in and mother him since our mother wasn't there.

Traits: Loves caring for people and animals. She has a soft spot for anyone or anything who is wounded. Loves giving people gifts. Makes sure her loved ones are safe, healthy, and nurtured. Can baby them at times. Puts others above herself. Feels bad for all injured and abandoned animals and children. Likes to write meaningful cards and letters to people she cares about.

How is she useful? As her mom became less competent, she took on her role. She's great at anticipating the needs of others. She's a great counselor, listener, friend, sister, wife, and mother. She's amazing in an emergency- she stays calm and handles any situation. She's a good cook and knows a lot about health and nutrition.

How is she self-defeating? She tends to help others at the expense of herself. She gives too much, then gets frustrated when no one gives to her. She has historically chosen men who were wounded and needy- men that reminded her of her brother subconsciously (emotionally wounded). She can't pass an injured animal without taking it home. She finds her thoughts frequently go to how to help others versus thinking about herself and her life.

What are her needs? She needs to put herself first every day. She needs rest and a spa day. She needs to let others be responsible for themselves and their happiness. She needs firm boundaries when people want too much from her or when they attempt to drain her energy. She needs to refrain from giving suggestions to those who may need them but aren't interested in them (even if they ask).

Biggest fear: That others will always come first and take up all her time.

False narrative: Others can't live their best life without my help and assistance.

WHAT'S NEXT

What was this experience like for you? Did you realize there were so many different "facets" to you? It is critical that we do not judge our facets, even if they are seemingly awful. They *all* developed for a reason, and those reasons were to keep you safe and intact. Sometimes I talk to clients who hate some of their facets. One that comes to mind was named "Emo Girl." She was shy, lazy, morbid, overly emotional, and didn't care about her appearance. She cut on herself regularly. My client wanted to kill off this facet, but we can never do that. What she didn't recognize was that Emo Girl was holding the experience of being sexually abused to keep it from contaminating the rest of the facets. She had such a big job and couldn't do it on her own, which was why she cut. She was also holding not only the memories of it but all of the emotions as well. She was literally the strongest and most caring facet to even dare take on this role. When my client was able to come to the rescue her whole life changed for the better.

Just like in Part 1, it is crucial to get to know each of these facet spinoffs intimately. Who are they and why did they develop? What are they holding for you? What are they angry about? Sad about? How do they try and get their needs met? What ARE their needs? Part of parenting these parts of you is determining what your facets' *true* needs are versus what they think they need. Another important aspect is learning how to love these parts of you unconditionally. This is the TRUE unconditional love we search for. The irony is only *we* can give it to ourselves.

MORNING ROUTINE

Let's add these facets to your morning ritual. It's helpful to list them all on one sheet of paper that you look at daily. Get creative! Many of my clients like to color code it and list out the top needs of each facet. There is no wrong way to create your facet sheet.

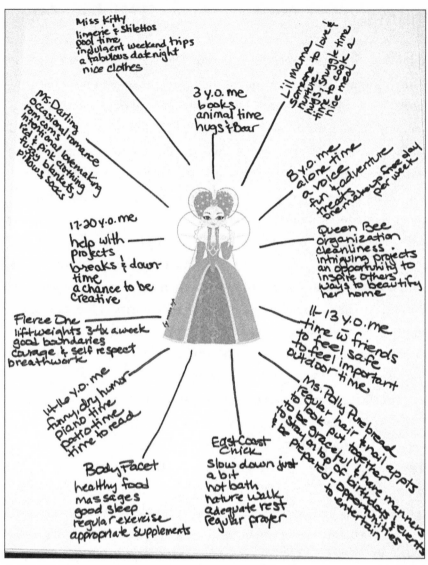

Miss Kitty
lingerie & stilettos
pool time
indulgent weekend trips
a fabulous date night
nice clothes

L'il mama
someone to love
nurture to cook
hugs, snuggle time a
time nice meal

3 y.o. me
books
animal time
hugs & Bear

Ms. Darling
occasional romance
rom coms
intentional lovemaking
red & pink clothing
fuzzy blankets
pillows socks

8 y.o. me
alone time
a voice
fun & adventure
treats make up one day
per week

Queen Bee
organization
cleanliness
intriguing projects
an opportunity to
inspire others
ways to beautify
her home

17-20 y.o. me
help with
projects
breaks & down-
time
a chance to be
creative

Fierce One
liftweights 3-4x a week
good boundaries
courage & self respect
breathwork

11-13 y.o. me
time w friends
to feel safe
to feel important
outdoor time

14-16 y.o. me
funny, dry humor
piano time
patio time
time to read

Ms. Polly Purebread
regular hair & nail appts
to look put together
to stay graceful & have manners
be on top of birthday & events
prepared - opportunities to entertain

East Coast
Chick
slow down just
a bit
hot bath
nature walk
adequate rest
regular prayer

Body Facet
healthy food
massages
good sleep
regular exercise
appropriate supplements

Facet Sheet Example

Hopefully, you are including prayers or gratitude in your morning spiritual practice. I want you to check in with **all** of your facets. Some may be quiet at first but over time they will connect with you and tell you what they need to be peaceful and joyful. I want you to see them as all being your children because they are. They are literally the most precious people in your life, and no one will love them more or better than you. You are going to give them the love, compassion, understanding, and guidance that they need and perhaps have never gotten. This may be the biggest undertaking of your life, but the reward is astounding!

Did some of you bristle when I said they are the most precious people in your life? I can hear you now. "No, my actual children are more precious," or "my spouse is the most important person to me." It may feel that way now, but that is likely born out of codependency, which we will talk about in a bit. In order to integrate trauma, you *must* be the center of your own universe, but not in an egotistical, narcissistic way. You must put your needs first during this process, otherwise something else will always get in the way. You may need to spend a little more time away from your family as you do these exercises. You may have to tell your children they are eating leftovers because you are working on yourself. You may need to start going to bed earlier, because this is grueling work at times that eats up a lot of bandwidth.

Look at it like this: If the BEST version of you can raise your children, that's the biggest gift you can give them. If the BEST version of you is married to your spouse, that is also the biggest give you can offer. Healing trauma means you no longer pass on the dysfunctions you were raised with. You show up in the world empowered. Your daughter will never overhear you complaining about your "fat thighs" because you love yourself way too much to ever utter those words. She also won't overhear you crying in the closet when life gets complicated.

YOUR INNER SUPERHERO

A NEW FACET

SO FAR, ALL THE FACETS YOU HAVE CREATED HAVE BEEN SUBCONSCIOUS. Now it's time to create from a place of **intention.** All your facets need a fearless leader. An inner CEO who is equal parts intelligent, kind, firm, loving, confident, and more. A TRUE SUPERHERO. This is where it gets fun!

CREATING YOUR INNER SUPERHERO

Creating an inner superhero can be an invaluable practice in helping you integrate more positive traits and behaviors into your being. This is the facet who will be in charge of all of your other facets. What traits does he/she need to possess to get this job done? Get creative! Close your eyes and picture him/her. Don't be shy! My inner superhero is 5'10" and has long, jet black hair. She only wears leather and latex, and she carries a riding crop. Her stilettos are never less than 6" and she rocks them!

Name: _____

Physical Description:

_____

_____

_____

_____

_____

Character Traits:

_____

_____

_____

_____

_____

How will your inner superhero help you honor the facets of you
and stop living in survival mode?

_____

_____

_____

_____

_____

What will you do/wear to remind yourself that your inner super-hero is present and with you?

_____

_____

_____

_____

_____

What is the new and truthful narrative your Inner Superhero lives by?

_____

_____

_____

_____

_____

How are you doing with this exercise? Was it easy? Difficult? If you are stuck, it's possible that your trauma occurred early in life before you had a chance to individuate from Mom and Dad. When this happens, we have difficulties cultivating an independent identity. You can do this; it just may take time and additional effort. Think about who you are apart from anyone else in your life, including your children, spouse, and other family. I know it's a morbid thought, but if they were all gone tomorrow who would you be?

Now that you have your newest facet, we must embody him/her. We start dressing like her, even if it's just a slightly bigger heel and a darker shade of lipstick. Maybe you buy a ring, watch, or other piece of jewelry that she has picked out. If you're a man doing this exercise, get creative. Maybe there's a tattoo that resonates, or perhaps your Inner Superhero has facial hair. Maybe you even change your hair style or color? Let's take this process seriously. After all, this is who you were meant to be all along.

Does that surprise you? It shouldn't. This is your highest self. THIS is who the Good Lord wanted you to be, but you had to earn it. God makes warriors by putting us through war. Read that again. You could never be your best self if life was a bowl of cherries. Does that mean I'm glad you are a trauma victim? Of course not! All trauma stinks. I would never wish upon anyone to be an abuse survivor, or to be impaired physically. I wouldn't even wish the "little" traumas upon anyone, like losing a job, or spraining an ankle. But what I learned after half a century of this work is that nothing introduces us to our own power more than trauma and hardship. It can be our best friend, or our biggest foe and **we** have decided to let it be our greatest catalyst for change and healing.

The alternative is we stay in the trauma cycle, which means we may do well for a bit and then the undertow comes and sweeps us away. We keep choosing the wrong partner. We are never able to lose that 10, 25, 50 or even 100 pounds. We can't finish projects, or schooling. Over time, we become worn down with health issues. We can't seem to put down the cigarettes or vape pen. We keep getting called into the In N Out™ drive thru or liquor store on our way home from work. Life feels like it's always against us, like we are always swimming upstream.

Here's where it gets interesting. Many of us *think* we want to break the trauma cycle, but so much of our identity is wrapped up in it that we are often scared to relinquish this identity. Who would we be without it? Who are we when we dismantle the stories we have crafted about our lives? What's left? Many don't have the courage to face this reality, and so stay stuck in the cycle even though they complain about it, ad nauseam.

Jessica's Story

Not long ago, I had a client referred to me by her physician. *Jessica was in her late 60s and had heart and liver disease. She needed to lose a good 50 pounds. I explained to her how I work, combining nutrition counseling with mind/body work for the best results. I told her I specialized in how trauma reacts in the body and that we would need to dig to figure out why she was emotionally eating and not able to drop the weight. She was on board-at first.

As soon as we got to the facets exercise, she changed her tune. "I didn't sign up for counseling," she said one day during our session. I had just reiterated how important it was to stick to the plan since she had been binging on several foods. She was also using chocolate whey protein because she didn't like the taste of the detox shake I had put her on. Instead of asking for ways to make it more palatable, she went rogue and added the chocolate. When I let her know this was not ok, she exploded. She told me I was critical, rigid, and made her feel small. I had struck a nerve. In the mental health world, we call this transference. It was clear she was talking to a parent or caregiver from her past and not to me. One of her facets had taken over as a means of protection (and perhaps rebellion), but we couldn't have that conversation because she didn't want to do the exercise. At the end of the session, she calmed down a bit and agreed to do "the counseling shit." I knew she wouldn't, and I was right. A few days later I got an email from her stating she no longer needed my services.

What's fascinating about Jessica was that she spent hours a day researching her conditions on the internet and sent me articles to read daily. She was always looking for a solution (and never trusted me or my process) but when it came to doing the hard work she ran. She was terrified. At almost 70 years old she was very steeped in her unhealed facet identity and her false narratives. She had no concept of cultivating her authentic self at that age and would rather keep herself stuck. Her consolation prize will be the binge eating and subsequent self-loathing that follows. Her real self didn't make these decisions, of course. It was a facet or a combination of facets. It just goes to show how powerful the facets can be.

I come across this resistance often in my work and in my personal life. Facing our traumas takes courage and it's a real commitment. We must be able to handle whatever it is we discover and be willing to *do the work*. Many clients bow out when I call them out for eating a chocolate bar. "It was in my drawer calling to me." When someone is diabetic and 80 pounds overweight AND has a chocolate bar in her drawer you know she is going to eat it. She also knows she is going to eat it, and if she was serious about changing, she would have thrown it out. Have you ever known a smoker to quit smoking with a pack of cigarettes in the drawer?

I see this a lot with sexual abuse survivors. They are often so traumatized they would rather keep the weight on so no one looks at them in a sexual manner and deal with the health consequences versus do the deep healing work of processing the trauma and reconnecting with their body. And so, they stay trapped inside themselves, literally.

TRAUMA AND ADDICTION/ CODEPENDENCY

LET'S TALK ABOUT TRAUMA AND ADDICTION. THEY SEEM TO GO HAND in hand and the potential addictions are many. Food, sex, gambling, work, shopping, screens, and people/love are a few I deal with on a regular basis. The mainstream usually refers to people addiction as "codependency" and for good reason. Some estimate that almost 90% of the population has codependency issues, which is staggering. There are several theories out there about codependency and each has merit. Codependency means getting your security or significance from another person. My friend Rene Eram, in his groundbreaking book *The Addict's Loop,* breaks down codependency into two roles: the Controller and the Dependent. The Controller is often the one who had to take on a lot of responsibility at an early age. They want to take on the role of solving the family's problems to feel safe and loved, even if this is largely unconscious. Usually, the Controller is trying to "fix" a Dependent, which is the people-pleaser who avoids confrontation. The Dependent feels entitled to be rescued from his broken life and the Controller is more than happy to rescue for a while.

At some point, the Controller gets angry when she realizes the Dependent is never going to rise up and take responsibility for himself. He isn't going to learn and integrate everything the Controller is teaching. If she gave him $500 and showed him how to balance his checkbook, it's just going to be a matter of time before he overdraws the account again, and he will have a new excuse every time. The Controller starts to get frustrated and becomes critical and insulting. Deep down the Dependent needs this to reinforce his low self-worth. The more the Controller lectures and criticizes, the more the Dependent will *seem* to try to please. But deep down he is still sabotaging himself because he *has to* reinforce the false identity of a weak, broken person.

Sounds exhausting, right? But how many of us have experienced this *very* thing? I hear about it a lot from female friends and clients who are almost always in the Controller role, though I see the opposite as well. Many women, especially trauma survivors, tend to look for "shelter pets" rather than equals in relationships. Think one-eyed, three-legged dogs. How many of us would take one in? They need all the love, right? They need someone to show them they are valuable and precious. And one-eyed dogs gaze at us (as best as they can) with a look of pure love and appreciation. It melts us. What would make a Controller feel more fulfilled than to be the one powerful enough to change that dog's life around? Do you see where this is going?

As the Controller, we get addicted to the quest of helping the other person rise up. And this doesn't have to be a mate-it could be a friend, sibling, or other family member. My sisters and I spent a lifetime trying to help my mother live a better life, only to be disappointed time and again when she chose cigarettes, junk food, and prescription pills over health.

As the Dependent, we get addicted to the strength of the Controller. It's a false sense of security for us. We also get addicted to pleasing the Controller, even though we secretly resent them and will find passive aggressive ways to "get back" at them for the put downs and controlling nature.

Rene says these roles are inherited and conditioned during childhood. They are chosen for us before we are even born. Whether you fit into the Controller or Dependent role, give yourself some grace. Keep in mind if you're an addict, you can easily take on both roles depending on the circumstance.

Here is a handout someone shared with me 15 years ago that I still look at regularly. It's spot on regarding codependency. Note which side you fall on and with whom?

When I feel responsible **FOR** others...	When I feel responsible **TO** others...
I fix...	I am...
protect	empathetic
rescue	encouraging
control	compassionate
carry their feelings	a great listener
don't listen	confrontational when needed
I feel...	I feel...
tired	unburdened
anxious	aware
fearful	empowered
liable/responsible	free
angry/frustrated	light
disgusted	unencumbered
I am concerned with...	I am concerned with...
the solution	relating to the other person
providing answers	discussing their feelings
details	**ALLOWING THE PERSON TO HAVE**
performance	**HIS OWN EXPERIENCE**
I manipulate and/or shame others to do what I think they should do	I firmly believe if I just offer moral support the other person has enough to make it through her crisis
I expect others to live up to **MY** expectations ☹	I only give advice when asked
	I allow the other person to be responsible for himself
	I **TRUST** and let go ☺

One of the most difficult things for a Controller is to let go of being responsible for other people. It can be terrifying. Notice which facets feel the need to be caretakers, and have your Inner Superhero intervene to make sure we don't keep falling into the same trap. We can NEVER live our best lives until we break the curse of codependency, which is yet another remnant of trauma.

TRAUMA AND SUBSTANCE ABUSE

It's obvious to most of us that becoming addicted to food, alcohol, drugs, tobacco, etc., is often the result of unintegrated and unresolved trauma. Life overwhelms us for one reason or another and we begin to rely on substances to make us feel better, to make us focus, or to stuff down our emotions. Sometimes, if we are really far gone, we want to numb out completely. These are your everyday heroin addicts, crack addicts, chronic alcoholics, and serious binge eaters. When they go into the "zone" they are lost. They can't hear the voices or cries of the facets begging for attention or wailing about the past.

I once had a friend who described his ex-wife's alcoholism like this:

> She had a 'special place' she could go to with the exact right number of drinks and cigarettes. It was always at least 10 drinks. When she got there, she lit a cigarette, took a puff, and closed her eyes. She was gone. She looked so peaceful, l and I was glad she could find comfort, even though she was ruining her body. She had a wistful look, and I was almost jealous of it at times. She spoke about her 'special place' like it was a serene beach on a desert island, and I didn't want to take that from her.

It was clear his wife needed peace and serenity, and this was the only way she knew how to get it. I had met this woman several times and she did not strike me as peaceful. She spoke loudly and made inappropriate jokes often at other peoples' expense. She permed her hair into very tight curls and looked and acted like she had been electrocuted. She was frenetic. I don't know much about her past, but it was obvious she was escaping from *something*. It made sense to me why she would need serenity.

Our facets are created to help us cope. Sometimes we cope by escaping, either literally or figuratively. We can't fault a facet for wanting to escape and feel better, but we must determine which facet/s have the addiction and we *must* parent them. Many times, a behavior that worked in the past is no longer productive now. We must bring our facets into present time and let them know the addiction or behavior is no longer acceptable. This is the job of your Inner Superhero.

Note: As I sit here writing, I have eaten a small bowl full of berries and half a protein bar. I still have the urge to munch. When I check in with myself, some of my facets are done with sitting at the computer (it's been 8 hours). I negotiated with them to hold on for one more hour and then we will go do something rejuvenating. Almost instantly, the urge to munch has subsided.

Years ago, I was a counselor at a methadone clinic. One of my mentors gave me a great insight. He said, "Addiction is always about ambivalence. Part of them wants to quit, and part of them doesn't. Whichever part is bigger, wins." He was spot on, yet he only scratched the surface. If I had discovered facets at that time my counseling approach would have been much different. What I did realize is that many of my clients thought and behaved like children- they were stubborn, emotional, rebellious, immature, and made poor decisions. Working with them was largely about helping them grow up. Their unhealed, immature facets had way too much power and were running the show. Imagine trying to take an ice cream cone away from a five-year-old and you'll get the picture.

Whether we are addicted to ho-hos or heroin, the pull is great. Sometimes even with our Inner Superhero in charge it's a challenge. It helps to get really clear on the why. *WHY* do you want to overcome your addiction? How would it enhance your life? What kind of life do you want to live? Can you become your best self with an addiction?

Many times, when I am working with a client, we come across a facet who is hell-bent on self-sabotage. Sam, age 48, had everything going for him. A second wife who adored him, a great job, a healthy child, and a nice home. His wife had become busy with work, and he started to feel ignored. Instead of addressing this with her, he started flirting with a young woman at work-a *much* younger woman. She happened to be 21 and in an entry level position. He was a manager. What's fascinating about this case is that he insists he was only slightly attracted to the young woman and had difficulty getting an erection both times they had intercourse.

He tried to cut the relationship off after several months, but the woman went off the rails. She contacted Sam's wife and shared their text messages, which devastated his wife. Consequently, she was referred to me by a friend. He nearly lost everything; for what? A woman he wasn't even attracted to? I knew this was deep facet work.

Sam's wife Colleen was your typical high-functioning trauma survivor. She could run circles around everyone and with two advanced degrees she was at the top of her game at work. She had a reputation of taking no shit. She was your quintessential Controller type. Sam was good at his job but had never finished college. He wasn't great with money and wasn't a leader at home, often relying on Colleen's strength.

Before he even did the facet work, I called him out. I explained a part of him didn't feel worthy of Colleen and how wonderful she was, and so he was going to sabotage the marriage because deep down he didn't think he deserved her. I also pointed out there may be another part (facet) that was resentful of her accomplishments and was going to passive aggressively "punish" her by cheating behind her back with a woman so below his own station so he could feel like a man. Both were speechless. I normally don't go that deep during a first session, but I wanted to test him to see if he was willing to do the hard work of facing the truth about himself and the wax-on wax-off process of integration.

I couldn't stop there. I pointed out to Colleen that "part" of her chose a Dependent because he was safe and wouldn't try to control her like her last husband. Now it was her chance to run the show. She owned it. It doesn't mean she deserved to be cheated on, but it explains how she found herself in that kind of mess.

At the end of the first session, I found out both of them smoked cigarettes. I told them I could not work with them unless they quit immediately. Normally, I would work on a quit plan with them, but I wanted to jolt them into realizing how hard this work would be. I also wanted them to put some real skin in the game up front.

One of the most important life lessons I have learned is **to never care more or work harder than the other person.** This goes for all kinds of relationships including marriage, friendships, relationships with family members, and even counselor/client. It is the crux of codependency. Whenever I break this cardinal rule, I always find myself holding the shorter end of the stick and that is **not ok**. If we find ourselves consistently working harder or showing up more it is coming from a dark place, most likely a wounded facet. Figure out which facet needs to feel loved and worthy and then do that deep parenting work. Tell her and show her she is loved. Find a photo of her and talk to her daily. Buy her a gift. Hug her. Have you ever hugged yourself? It feels delightful! Take her on a walk, paint her nails, show up for HER like you do for everyone else. This is the key.

> **Note:**
> Cigarettes are often a replacement for a mother's love. Perhaps your mother was cold and distant? Perhaps she was smothering? Either way, we will often gravitate towards smoking when we have unresolved issues with Mom. Sucking is one of our first instincts to feel comfort. If you are a smoker, ask yourself why you are reverting to infancy to get your needs met? The answer may surprise you.

OTHER ADDICTIONS

Just because you aren't binging on Oreos or blowing smoke rings doesn't mean you don't have an addiction. Take a long, hard look. Do you overspend? Are you living paycheck to paycheck? I hear this a lot and I also hear the excuses- inflation, kids' activities, the price of gas. The reality is many people do not say no to their facets enough and do not practice enough discipline to save money. The same person who tells me she is "broke" has hair extensions, fake fingernails, a $500 handbag, and subscribes to every movie channel known to man.

Do you scroll on your phone a bunch? How often do you look at porn? If you do, does your spouse know? Do you gamble?

Donna's Story

Last year I worked with a woman who was referred to me for weight loss. When I read her bio and met *Donna, I learned about her painful past and several traumatic events, including being married to a highly abusive man for nearly two decades. I also learned she was in recovery for a severe gambling addiction and had lost nearly a million dollars. She *almost* lost her very patient and caring second husband over it.

We got through the first part of the facet exercise, and she mentioned needing to clean her room. I asked her to send me pics and when she did, I realized that I needed to intervene right away. She had signs of hoarding and we were never going to make progress with her in that much chaos. Luckily, she only lived a few miles away, so we scheduled a Saturday for me to show up and help her get her room organized. I also wanted to assess the rest of the house.

It was evident Donna was also addicted to "stuff." Nearly every room was cluttered with piles and stacks and the further you got into the house the worse it became. Her bedroom was piled high with clothes, shoes, bathroom supplies, papers, magazines- all the makings of a good hoarder. Lots of the clothes still had tags, and several pairs of shoes were still brand new and in boxes.

When I started a donate pile, Donna became nervous. I can't tell you how many times I heard her say, "No, I want to keep that." She was even uncomfortable with me throwing away an old chapstick when she had a dozen. I realized she needed a warm, authoritative figure and since she had not yet created her Inner Superhero I decided to step in and be that for her.

As the day wore on, she began trusting me more and more. We took six large garbage bags of trash out of her room, and another five for the local Goodwill. It was obvious she was not in her adult facets as often as she needed to be, and she didn't have a clue as to how to parent her immature facets and stop them from ruining her life.

After we cleaned her room, Donna got inspired to clean other parts of the house. She organized her office and desk and got her dirty clothes off the floor and into hampers. When we would have our sessions, she would start crying within the first 30 seconds and I would parent her sad, scared facets, giving them encouragement and unconditional positive regard. It's important to note that on top of a very abusive first husband, Donna had a highly critical mother that (in my opinion) was the crux of her real trauma. She never hugged Donna or told her that she loved her. Both of her parents were alcoholics, and Donna was the oldest child. Add onto that sexual abuse starting at age seven and no wonder Donna was still so traumatized.

*It's important to note that hoarding is often a result of sexual trauma and abuse. I saw this in my own mother, and my theory is that the excess stuff helps the traumatized person feel more grounded. Trauma can create dissociation, on a small scale or a large scale. I felt that Donna probably dissociated while eating, gambling, and buying things to some degree and it would just get worse over time. Conversely, eating can also make us feel more grounded, especially if we are eating large quantities of heavy foods like burgers, fries, mashed potatoes, prime rib, anything fried, etc. **Trauma survivors often look for ways to be grounded and escape their pain at the same time.**

Unfortunately, Donna did not continue her work with me. She got to the first part of Facets part 2 and dropped off. This happens a lot, and it still makes me sad because we had so much work left to do. But I can't want it more for someone than she wants it for herself, and so I move on but almost always leave the door open. I imagine Donna was scared to look at her spinoff facets because some of them were most likely dark and powerful. It's also possible she was afraid they would go away and then she wouldn't be able to sneak back into her coping skills when she felt the urge.

> **Note:**
> Donna spent hundreds of dollars each month on Doterra products. I tried to explain gently that her health conditions were not going to improve with these oils and that she needed to do the hard work. I asked if she could limit herself to one oil a month and she said, "no way." She bought into a fantasy that she could ward off illness with these oils even though her CRP (C-Reactive Protein), an inflammation marker, was over 32. Doterra certainly isn't going to fix that and deep down she knew it. She was not ready to face the truth.

CHAPTER

TRAUMA AND EATING DISORDERS

EATING DISORDERS ARE A BITCH. THEY ARE A BITCH TO HAVE, AND they are a bitch to treat. I would almost rather treat a murderer than someone with anorexia because at least the serial killer has more self-worth to kill others versus himself. Give me five sex addicts any day over one client with an eating disorder. That's how dark the disorder is.

Most people who struggle with an eating disorder are kind and wonderful people. The difference between your average "soft" addiction and an eating disorder is that people with an eating disorder usually want to die. At least some of their facets do. Sigmund Freud referred to this as the Thanatos instinct, or the death instinct. He said everyone had it to some degree. This is why you can be driving 60 MPH down a two-lane road and when you see a car coming from the opposite direction you have a flash of what it would be like to crank the wheel and collide head on with the other car.

You might argue that a drug addict also has a strong Thanatos instinct, and you may be correct. In my experience, the instinct tends to be stronger in those with an eating disorder, particularly Anorexia Nervosa.

ANOREXIA NERVOSA

One of my favorite clients of all time is a young woman named Jillian. I had been seeing her father for some time for his own issues with anxiety and he mentioned his 15-year-old daughter had been put in the Eating Disorder Unit at the local Children's Hospital. She had wasted away to nothing and was having heart trouble, swelling, and a host of other problems. She was in the hospital for some time, and shortly after she came out, he started bringing her to sessions with me. Since I'm also a nutritionist, we thought I could reach her on several levels. She expressed a strong interest in nutrition and health, and I was hoping I could inspire her to focus her desire to help others onto herself as well.

When I first met Jillian, I thought she was radiant. Perfect. If I had a daughter, I would want her to be just like Jillian. She was beautiful, smart, sweet, and opinionated. She had a stubborn streak and she beat to her own drum. She was clearly a magical, mythical creature. I couldn't imagine this young woman self-loathing enough to starve herself.

When I took her history and asked about her life it was clear she felt stifled. She was the younger of two girls who lived at home with her parents, sister, and maternal grandmother who had been in a terrible car accident and was paralyzed from the neck down. Mom and Grandma ran a business on their property that Jillian's older sister was a part of, but Jillian had no interest. She felt a rift between her and her mother, and stated she was much closer to her father.

Both parents were super over-achievers. They were not money-driven but highly accomplishment-oriented. Both worked hard in their careers, and dinner talk was almost always about work and accomplishments. I wasn't there, but it didn't sound like there was much talk about planning fun times or having adventurous experiences. Perhaps rather boring for a whimsical child, but would that alone cause an eating disorder?

There was one detail about dinner that struck me as odd. Jillian's mother was a stickler for table manners, and when Jillian was young, she would light three candles at the table. Every time Jillian would have bad manners at dinner, she would blow a candle out. If all three candles were blown out Jillian had to leave the table. On the surface this may seem like a clever way of teaching table manners, but I think it had the opposite effect. Children's brains are so impressionable, and I wondered if it was possible that extinguishing all three candles represented death on a Jungian, collective unconscious level, somehow activating Thanatos? I hadn't discovered facets at that time but perhaps it created a facet to hold shame, and this was the one who didn't want to live?

It was also fascinating that Jillian's dad held a great deal of shame about events that happened to him as a child. He was terribly bullied in school and there was one incident that was particularly traumatizing. He was in high school and on the football team, where some of the members bullied him regularly. One day he opened his locker to find human feces inside. I made him relive this with me and do a lot of integration work around it, but I can't imagine the horror of that moment. If it happened to me, I think I would want to disappear. Was there any way he passed that shame onto his daughter? They were, in fact very close- too close, and I explained how damaging that can be to a developing girl. She lived on a farm, was highly sheltered, and didn't have enough positive peer experiences, in my opinion.

I worked with Jillian for several years. I also worked with her parents. They needed to learn how to let her be her own person yet put appropriate boundaries in place. Mom needed to stop being hypercritical, and Dad needed to stop coddling. What I loved (and still love) about this family is that they were willing to do the work. Mom had grown up with a lot of poverty and challenges and was a no-nonsense woman. Even though she was polished and well-read, she would put her boots and jeans on and work the farm from sunup to sundown. She was assertive yet worked hard to bite her tongue and let Jillian be herself.

Mom and Dad also worked on their relationship. Dad had difficulty communicating without getting heated (something he passed on to Jillian) and he and his wife both had to learn the art of negotiating.

If I was working with this family now, I would introduce the Facet work and I think it would make a huge impact. It would have been helpful to see how the facets all interacted with each other. I would have loved to dive into Mom's "Miss Manners" facet, and Dad's "Ashamed Adolescent" facet. Of course, I would have loved to get to know Jillian's "Disappearing Act" facet and let her know that she is absolutely supposed to be on this Earth.

The good news is this family is thriving. Jillian graduated college and is a professional athlete and coach. She is in a loving, stable relationship. Mom and Dad are doing well, also. They let Jillian do her own thing and Mom and Jillian are close. We still keep in touch.

Many people say Anorexia is about control, and often it is. Unfortunately, there can be a deep self-loathing involved when one is restricting food to this degree. Often, this is due to how the child is raised. Perhaps a controlling parent made them feel like they did not have the intelligence to individuate and start making their own decisions? It's possible that being sexually abused makes a child feel such shame that they don't feel like they matter enough to exist, or they are so embarrassed they literally want to "disappear."

Conversely, there can also be a deep sense of self-preservation. Notice how most Anorexia develops in adolescence, when one is in the Identity versus Identity Confusion stage (see Erickson's Psychosocial Stages of Development Theory). Restricting food can be a self-protective measure to avoid conforming to the parents' wishes and therefore altering the core identity. The sentiment is, "self-preservation at all costs."

What this equates to is that even if the afflicted person dies, they are dying with their true identity intact.

I sensed this could have been more the case with Jillian. She had always been a bit on the stubborn side in childhood and wanted to remain a pink unicorn in a family of Clydesdales. It wasn't safe for her to be a unicorn, and perhaps this was her version of teenage rebellion.

> **Note:**
> Often, when I am working with someone with Anorexia Nervosa, I notice that they are either not brought up with any kind of faith or are raised in a stern, overly religious environment. For those with no faith, it can be more challenging in recovery when they don't believe in anything greater than themselves, and they see how sick they are. I always encourage them to explore spirituality in whatever form they are drawn to.

BULIMIA NERVOSA

Many eating disorders overlap these days which makes it challenging to get to the core issues. Recently, I saw an article where actress Tess Holliday claimed her main diagnosis is Anorexia. This seems odd considering she is morbidly obese, but these days when a person is diagnosed with an eating disorder it is rarely just one disorder. Many people with bulimia also have phases where they are anorexic. Some anorexics are also diagnosed with Binge Eating Disorder, even if they are only binging on cucumbers. Tess claims she has *atypical* anorexia and low body weight does not need to be one of the symptoms.

I tend to look at eating disorders differently from others in the mental health community. In my opinion, eating disorders are almost always a spiritual crisis as the result of unintegrated intense trauma. The spiritual crisis comes from the core identity being stunted due to any set of circumstances that interrupted its development. The developmental facets are seriously interrupted, and the spinoff facets will be complicated.

When we experience trauma as an adult, we often have some healthy coping mechanisms in place to process and cope. When we experience trauma in childhood, the earlier the trauma the more likely it is going to arrest development, create spinoff facets, and block our relationship with any kind of higher power.

When we experience trauma before we have started to individuate from our parents, serious identity issues can arise. We normally start individuating from parents around age four, when we become aware that we are not sharing a brain with Mom and Dad. This is usually when kids begin lying, and it's a healthy part of development. Kids begin to lie when they realize their parents cannot read their thoughts. They become conscious of the fact that they are their own little people.

I don't think I would have ever truly understood this concept if I hadn't experienced it myself, firsthand. Being abducted from my mother at age three, I hadn't reached any kind of individuation. I was completely in love with my mother, as all toddlers should be. I beamed every time she smiled at me and thought she was a fairy princess. I also thought I was connected to her, somehow. She was my higher power and I relied on her for everything.

All of that changed in one swift moment. When I was taken away, I became hysterical and the hole I felt in my chest was all-encompassing. As the days and weeks wore on, I felt like I was living with the pause button on. I was getting through the days but had little joy. I was haunted by my mother's face, her scent, and secretly obsessed about her. Every time I left the house, I stared at every woman with dark hair hoping she was my mother. My emotional development all but stopped. Instead of enhancing my core identity, I developed spinoff facets. Some of these facets were mature, especially the mother facet who cared for my baby brother (who was also abducted). But these facets developed out of necessity *not* normalcy and were not truly who I was supposed to be.

Consequently, this is where codependency is born. All codependency is stunted development. We rely on outside sources for our security and significance because we are too undercooked for it to emanate from within.

Rachel's Story

Last year I started working with a beautiful young woman named *Rachel. She was married with three kids and was a stay-at-home mom. She loved her family and her life, but she was filled with anxiety and was overwhelmed with having three kids all under the age of six. She was having chronic headaches and stomach aches and just never felt good. She was also frequently exhausted.

When I read her bio, I discovered she had been sexually abused by a close family friend beginning at age four. She never told her parents and repressed the memories until she went off to college. Shortly after leaving home some of the memories returned and hit her like a freight train. She was so depressed she couldn't leave her bed. She had to return home and process her memories. She had several binge-eating experiences in high school but once the memories came back permanently, she started binging like crazy. She would binge to the point of involuntary vomiting and then keep eating.

Binge-eating is powerful because it accomplishes several things. First, it temporarily quells whatever pain we are feeling by indulging in the opposite feeling of euphoria. We keep eating because we cannot get enough euphoria because the pain spring is endless. It's constantly going off like Old Faithful and when it spouts it can be debilitating. This is where binge-eating and sex/porn addiction are similar; it's the intense pleasure that is temporarily dulling the pain.

The other reason binge-eating is so powerful is that it gives us a false sense of feeling grounded. The food literally makes us feel heavy, and if we feel heavy, we won't float away. It's a rudimentary attempt to stay intact and prevent dissociation or depersonalization, two hindbrain (survival) responses to trauma that are still largely ignored, even today.

A third added benefit of binge-eating is that it can be a literal love replacement. Food is equated with love in many cultures. How many of us have had a mother or grandmother who nursed our hurts with food? Rich, fatty, sugary foods can release powerful chemicals in our bodies that make us feel loved and safe. In my practice, I find clients believe ice cream is the perfect self-medicating food-rich, creamy, sugary, and chock full of fat. On top of that, it's easier to purge, according to the bulimics I have worked with.

Rachel was experiencing all of these temporary comforts and more. Even the purge cycle has a little-known benefit. Most people don't discuss it, but purging is a hindbrain response to getting rid of something poisonous. It's a true survival instinct gone awry. Often, in the case of trauma, a person is trying to rid themselves of the toxic experience(s) and this is the body's only way of knowing how to do it. In a sense it's the body performing a self-exorcism, only it doesn't work long-term and just perpetuates the shame cycle until the next binge. Perhaps subconsciously they feel like if they purge enough times, eventually they will rid themselves of the poison, even if they throw their guts up in the process. This is not a logical process, and we cannot fault the client for this behavior. It is deeply instinctual and often takes drastic action to stop. Some now equate the vagus nerve to trauma responses, but this is only scratching the surface. There are several parts that make up the "hind brain" and they all work in conjunction to ensure survival. In the medulla alone there are four types of cranial nerves (including the vagus nerve) that all have to do with the mouth, gag reflexes, and taste sensations.

In the pons, there are four types of cranial nerves as well, including the abducens nerve, which coordinates eye movements. It's no surprise that Rachel had issues with her eyes tracking in grade school and needed rather extensive eye therapy to correct it.

The fact is, for many the binge/purge cycle does seem to work in the beginning. Over time, it takes more and more cycles to feel any sense of comfort until it has the complete opposite effect and then the client must spend the day in bed convalescing after eight binge purge cycles in one day. Sounds like drug addiction, right? This tends to be the case with many faulty coping skills-they always turn on us over time. Stopping them feels like trying to crawl out of the pits of hell with demons holding our feet down. For many it is nearly insurmountable.

When we discovered Rachel's facets it was easy to see which ones were prone to the binge-purge cycle.

"Slothra" was developed when Rachel was around 17 years old.

Traits: Lazy, avoids, sabotages, wants immediate pleasure and comfort rather than dealing with emotions or problems. Wants to check out, gets depressed easily, enjoys binge-watching television and eating sweets. Doesn't like getting dressed or putting on makeup.

Triggers: Having to function.

How is she useful? "Protects in the moment by checking out when I just need to keep functioning."

How is she self-defeating? Makes it hard to get anything done. Also makes it hard to deal with emotions. Sabotages through food choices.

What are her needs? Surface: Permission to check out Core: Comfort and safety.

What is her biggest fear? Having to face reality.

What is her false narrative? "I can't do life. I'm not equipped."

Often, when clients come across facets with these traits, they want to kill them off. Slothra is a force to be reckoned with. She has a lot of power and doesn't usually make good choices. She's the main binger, and with good cause: she's not mature enough to handle the gravity of Rachel's traumatic past. Checking out is the best coping skill she has to keep from going insane. The truth is, Slothra is holding the trauma of the abuse, and it's a task too large to bear. It's so heavy all she can do is lie around and check out. Rachel's psyche created her out of a "lazy teenager" developmental stage and basically handed her the memories of abuse to keep on lock down. What a giant task for such an ill-equipped little girl. The psyche will do this at times to keep the other facets intact and to keep Rachel as a whole surviving and functioning. It was Slothra's job to "take over" whenever there was a threat of a memory surfacing so as not to let Rachel descend into madness. From Slothra's standpoint it would be better to stay in her little bubble versus experience life and risk a descent into madness.

In addition to other "healthier" facets like Mother, Fashionista (the creative one), Star (the spiritual one) and Monica (the clean freak) Rachel's psyche also created

Mentella around age 21.

Traits: Wild hair that looks like she's been electrocuted, hospital gown in a psych-ward look, holds the rage, likes to have control, trusts no one, hates religion, will put people in their place, loses her temper a lot.

Triggers: Any perceived injustice.

How is she useful: Helps me have control, forces me to use my voice, keeps me and my family safe

How is she self-defeating: "Can explode in anger, keeps me alone, can be too fearful and acts out of fear at times."

What are her needs? Surface: control and for things to be dealt with. Couch time. Core: comfort and a voice.

What is her biggest fear? Total loss of control. Injustice.

What is her false narrative? "I cannot trust that anything is real or safe."

If we think about it, it makes sense that Rachel's psyche would create another spinoff to hold the rage of her trauma. Pain and rage are too much for one facet to hold, and so the logical thing to do is split off again. Mentella seemed scary to Rachel at first, but I assure you, she is a distinctly valuable facet. It is appropriate to carry rage when one is sexually abused, and it is quite a task. Of *course*, Mentella looked like she had been electrocuted- in a sense she had been. Once she was created, she was handed all the rage at once, which would certainly frazzle any-one. She's holding all the fury of what happened to Rachel, and she may even be rageful that she is the only one carrying all of it. Unfortunately, for trauma survivors it takes a facet like this in order to be able to set boundaries with others. Often times, many of the other facets are too caring or codependent to stand up for themselves, and so we need a wild-haired Mentella to show us how it's done.

As I kept working with Rachel Slothra and Mentella became my favorite facets. It's often in the "yuck" where we find the buried trea-sure. These two facets needed some parenting and some polishing, but they were powerhouses. Rachel just needed to learn how to "tap in." She started by checking in with them every day to ask them what they needed. Slothra needed loads of downtime. Rachel couldn't give her "loads" with three small children, but she did start scheduling couch time where she could relax and watch a movie. Instead of calling it "check out time" we called it convalescing. In fact, that's truly what it was. Slothra was exhausted from carrying the trauma and she needed downtime to heal and recharge. She felt empowered being seen and having Rachel honor her. Slowly, her food cravings started to dissipate and when they would surface Rachel realized it was because Slothra wasn't getting her needs met. Eventually, Rachel started scheduling morning prayer and meditation time to help Slothra and Mentella become more balanced and process the trauma in a healthy way. Being proactive like this is a necessary part of trauma integration. Checking in with your facets daily is a key component in the healing process.

When it was time for Rachel to create her Inner Superhero, she had no trouble. Most clients come up with a completely separate name, but not Rachel. She said she had a higher self in there whom she correlated to her adolescent development self at age 18.

SUPERHERO RACHEL

Traits: Confident, social, enjoys a good time, loves her friends, desires independence, loves singing loudly, loves girls' night. Can speak her mind. Stands up for herself. Is a great parent and a loving wife. Sets boundaries. Wants to be her best self and live her best life. Appreciates her body. Is full of gratitude for her many blessings.

How she will help me: Higher-self Rachel is the inner CEO. She is in charge of all the other facets. She parents them with love and discipline and sets boundaries. She encourages them all. She checks in with them daily to see what they need. She makes sure they are all seen and heard.

What she needs: The only thing Rachel needs is dominion over the other facets. She needs to have the authority to "run the show." She is competent and capable, and she is the best one to make decisions.

Superhero Rachel does not have fear or needs. She gets her supply right from the source-Almighty God. Just like angels are not insecure when

God gives them wings, our higher self is not insecure about whether s/he can run our life. They have full faith and are our connection to the Divine. Remember, this is who you were meant to be all along. Sometimes we take the long way to get there, and it makes the journey all the more special. When Mentella is raging, Superhero Rachel can comfort her, problem-solve with her, and negotiate with her. Most of all, she can express gratitude to Mentella for being so dedicated and faithful to her duty of carrying rage and protecting the other facets. This is a task that indeed deserves angel wings.

CHAPTER

SEXUAL TRAUMA

Not long ago I had a dream. I was going to see a new chiroprac-tor and the assistant made me get into a hospital bed. Once I did, I was wheeled down into the basement. I was there for a while, before an-other assistant came along and wheeled me down a tunnel into another basement-type room that was more rustic and unfinished. I laid there for what seemed like hours, and finally started asking passers-by why I had been forgotten. "We haven't forgotten you," is all they would say as they hurried by. After what felt like forever, I finally got out of the bed and went to the front desk and asked to use the phone. I called my husband. He answered and was irritated that I wasn't home yet. I said, "Something has happened to me. I can't tell you now but please know it's not my fault and I'm on my way home." After I hung up, I realized I didn't have a purse or car keys, so I dialed him back and said, "I need your help. I don't have keys and I don't know where I am."

I woke up from this dream feeling empty. Due to my training, I know any dreams about a basement typically refer to the subconscious and I could sense something was in mine that needed to come out. The dream indicated that something was *deep* in there since I had been taken to a second basement. I was in a hospital bed, which represents injury. What's fascinating is that I got out of the bed and reached out to my husband, my one rock. "Something has happened to me," was a clear indicator that a memory was coming. I loved that I said it wasn't my fault and I also love that I called him back, telling him I needed his help. This is real progress for me.

The whole day after that dream I felt like I had been run over. Some of my facets wanted to dissociate and take over, but I didn't let them. I'm experienced enough to know these are the "labor" pains of birthing a new traumatic memory, so I let myself take it easy and just let it come on its own time. Normally, there would have been an urge to check out, either with food, wine, chocolate, or a nap. I'm good at resisting those urges these days, but surprisingly none came. I was fully ready for the experience.

I couldn't tell you exactly when the memory hit. It was like it came in sections. First, I got the message, "four months old." It played over and over like a broken record. I have had a peripheral memory of being sexually abused at four months old that came out when I was writing my first book. It was quite a surprise, and I didn't know what to do with it since it wasn't the focus of my writing, so I filed it away as something I would address later. That was nearly five years ago.

Four months, four months, four months. I wondered how I knew I had been abused at four months of age. I knew nothing of myself at that age except for one thing.

My mother had taken me to Sears Portrait Studio to get my picture taken when I was four months old. The only reason I know this is because I have a large 10x12 portrait of me smiling in a cute baby bonnet. Evidently, the picture won the store's cutest baby contest, and my mother always had that picture hanging of me wherever we lived.

One day I asked my mother how old I was in the photo. "About four months old," she replied. Somehow my subconscious filed that away for over 25 years. After the dream, I started getting flashes of things happening to me. They were a fraction of a second and I couldn't tell if they were real. Images of an old man with grey hair. Repeated flashes of him moving my diaper to the side and touching me, all the while hearing, "Four months old. Four months old."

I remembered a part of the dream when I was lying in the hospital bed. In the dream it occurred to me that maybe I should feel afraid. After all, I didn't know these people and I had no idea where I was. I felt the fear creeping in, and I instantly pushed it out. I felt nothing.

When I thought on it, I couldn't remember the last time I felt fear in my waking life. I still can't. At first, I thought maybe it was because I have great control over my facets. I have worked hard to conquer any and all fears over the years: driving, mountain lions, spiders, even wasps and hornets. I'm not a person that normally feels a lot of fear, but it is a normal human emotion, right?

As I sat with it, what I realized is that I am numb to fear. I have constructed the Berlin Wall to fear, and it never crosses. Somewhere along the line I decided it was the worst feeling on the planet and I blocked it out. On the surface, this may seem like a victory, but let's look deeper. Appropriate fear is healthy. Gavin de Becker wrote a book called, *The Gift of Fear*. It certainly serves its purpose. Why am I so unwilling to experience it?

A few days before the dream I was driving and was almost hit by another car. I had to slam on my brakes, and yet I felt no fear. Nothing. I knew it wasn't normal, yet after a few seconds I turned the radio up and went on my merry way. Why didn't I even have an increase in my heart rate?

Here is the problem. When we can't feel fear (or pain I might add), we also cannot experience joy. Blocking out negative emotions is a self-protective mechanism. Unfortunately, we throw the baby out with the bath water, and we relent to living a very black and white life in order to have a pain-free existence. What's ironic is, I have no problem feeling physical or emotional pain. It's fear that I can't seem to tolerate. At least my facets have all said no to it. I think they formed a union.

I wasn't quite sure what to do with this memory at first. My brain tried to connect the dots. Did the man who took my picture abuse me? Did my mother leave him alone with me to use the restroom? Did he choose me as the contest winner out of guilt or some sick fantasy? My mother is deceased, and I will never have the answer to these questions. All I can do is let my Inner Superhero Sparrow comfort all the facets of me that need it. If there is any way to feel the pain of it, I am committed to doing so. So far nothing has come except complete exhaustion and the emptiness. For several days after I birthed that memory, I fell asleep while sitting up. That is highly unlike me, but it's ok. I was convalescing.

It took several weeks to fully integrate that trauma. I can't say that I "let it go," because it happened and is a part of my fabric. But once I fully integrated it the memory stopped bombarding me and now when I think of it, it feels like it happened to someone else. There are no emotions or symptoms connected to the experience.

INTEGRATION

Integrating sexual trauma is one of the most complex healings on the planet. Sexual traumas are like acid rain snowflakes-no two situations are alike, but they all have their own brand of tragic. That experience and memory wasn't difficult for me to integrate because I already knew I was an abuse survivor. I was almost grateful for that memory as I believe it to be my earliest experience of abuse. To pull out a toxic root like that is an enormous blessing. Of course, I mourned for that four-month-old little girl who was completely powerless, but I am here to take care of her every day for the rest of my life.

For many, healing and integrating sexual abuse can take years, especially when we have built a foundation for ourselves out of trauma. We must unwind ourselves and our facets in order to integrate and commit to the healing process. It's often the most difficult thing a person does in life.

Sexual abuse creates huge problems with our developmental facets and is the catalyst for many spinoff facets. It changes who we are and who we are to become. It can be the core trauma related to many unhealthy behaviors, such as substance abuse, eating disorders, sex addiction, mental illness, and suicide. We learned from Rachel how early sexual abuse can nearly ruin our lives. No one knows this better than *Kyle.

Kyle's Story

Kyle* was a 54-year-old construction worker who came to see me for depression. He was wildly unhappy in his 30-year marriage to a seemingly normal woman who worked a government job. They had three grown kids together and Kyle had been having a torrid affair with a coworker named Ally*.

What was fascinating was that Kyle was a cross dresser. When he came to my office, he would visit the rest room to change into his female clothing, which included a polyester dress, prosthetic breasts, pantyhose, and heels. His choice in clothing looked like something a grandma would wear, but I didn't comment on it.

Kyle's bio was the stuff of nightmares. His father, a preacher, had accidentally killed Kyle's three-year-old brother in an accident involving his truck and went off the deep end. Within a few months he started dressing Kyle in his wife's clothes and sodomizing his own son. Kyle was around six at the time and was shocked this was happening. This went on rather frequently, every time his mother left home to run errands.

Kyle said after each occurrence his father would go about life pretending everything was fine. This went on for years. I asked Kyle how it came to an end. He replied, "Dad stopped when I started enjoying it."

This confession sent a shiver up my spine. How do you fault a little boy for acclimating to his environment? Kyle had begun stealing his mother's clothing and dressing up when no one was around. In some strange way it felt "right" for him to be dressed as a woman.

Fast forward to age 54 and Kyle is still dressing like his mother. Only now, he is sodomizing himself with sex toys. He was seeing Ally, who was questioning her own gender identity and was dressing like a man. She wore a prosthetic penis under her clothes and seemed like the "perfect" complement to Kyle's trans tendencies.

Kyle could not see the relationship between his father's abuse and his own self-inflicted torture. He saw it from the peripheral sense but couldn't really make the connection that he was just picking up where his father left off in the abuse department.

One part of Kyle's story I will never forget was how he told me that when he dressed in women's clothing, he literally saw a woman's body when he looked down at his feet, legs, and torso. When he looked in the mirror, however, the spell was broken, and he saw he had the face of a rugged man. I knew this must have had to do with his abuse and the fact that he may have looked down at himself often while his father was abusing him. Perhaps he bought into the fantasy that he was, indeed, a woman, so that he could make sense of what was happening to him? No doubt he had spinoff facets that developed to help him cope. Maybe more than one of them was female?

Another part that intrigued me was the fact that Kyle had tried to leave his wife on several occasions to go and live with his mistress. Each time he never lasted longer than a day before he panicked and returned home. His wife always welcomed him home and accepted his cross-dressing. She was even willing to overlook the mistress in exchange for keeping the marriage intact. She was invested in brushing all of Kyle's issues under the rug.

Shortly before Kyle stopped seeing me, he decided he wanted to try dating men. This was right when the internet dating sites were making their debut, and I think he had been perusing them. I tried to urge him to avoid making that decision while we were still working together because I didn't think he was actually gay (*and* he was married), but he seemed determined. Because he had been so traumatized and conditioned at an early age by a caregiver, being sodomized became his normal. I wonder if he would have had the same feelings in his "masculine" clothing? My guess is that if he tried to date a man dressed as a man the spell would have been broken, at least temporarily. I will never know.

Once again, I wish I had discovered facets while working with Kyle. Perhaps I would have gotten through to him on some level that he was just replaying his past over and over. Where was that little boy that was so traumatized? My guess is he was attached to his matronly wife, whom he couldn't be away from for more than a day and who always welcomed him back with open arms. She provided safety and comfort for him, which he seemed to need above all else. I hope he was able to find peace.

Processing sexual trauma often happens in layers. It's quite helpful to have the facets well established, along with our Inner Superhero so that we can create a safe space for the facets to heal and be heard.

Samara's Story

Trauma in the LGBT community is a sensitive topic. It's almost not politically correct to point out that many members of this community have physical, emotional, and/or sexual abuse in their history. The popular opinion is that they are "born this way." I have had many clients and friends over the years who were part of the LGBT community and in my experience, most of them had childhoods full of trauma, abuse, and dysfunction.

I met *Samara years ago sitting at the bar of a little Mexican restaurant. She was tall and looked like Sporty Spice in basketball shorts with her pulled hair up. She was drinking a beer and watching a game on the tv. I said hello and she barely glanced in my direction. I don't recall how we eventually struck up a conversation, but she informed me she was a teacher getting her master's in special education. I told her what I did for a living, and she immediately laughed and informed me she came from "the most fucked up family." I liked her instantly.

As the evening went on, Samara told me more about her life. She was married to a woman who lived across the country. She showed me a photo of a very overweight woman dressed scantily in pinup-type clothing with drag-queen level makeup on and carrying a chihuahua dressed as a ballerina. I was surprised to see this was Samara's choice in a partner since she was more of a sporty woman, but I learned this is often the case in lesbian relationships. It is not uncommon for one partner to completely turn away from her feminine side while the other partner lives almost entirely in hers. It was clear Samara was proud of her "wife" (they weren't legally married) and showed me several more photos.

Samara went on to explain that her wife *June had moved to the West Coast to "find herself" and that she hadn't seen her in over six months. Samara was at home raising one of June's sons, and regularly checked in on the other son. Samara worked several jobs in addition to teaching. Two nights a week she bartended and multiple days out of the week she refereed after school. She did this so she could pay June's expenses- rent, car payment, food, etc.

The more I heard the more shocked I was. I knew the stereotypes about lesbians, but I never had any close lesbian friends and I had never treated a lesbian client long-term in therapy. I couldn't believe what I was hearing. Samara was completely sacrificing her life for rights to claim a wife and received no benefit to being "married" other than two sons she adored and a stack full of bills.

Another drink in, I asked if June was a kind person. Samara started to shut down at this point, and I was almost sorry I had asked. I quickly changed the subject back to school. She didn't perk up like I was hoping, and actually said she was probably going to get kicked out because she was a tad short on tuition. I asked how much, and she told me-$900.

I looked at this woman and could see right through her. She grew up in a poor, Hispanic home. She was overweight and never felt pretty, so she found her feminine identity outside of herself in someone else. She had sacrificed everything she had just to keep that identity, including her pride and self-worth. I could tell no one had ever really shown up for her. I did something I have never done before. I reached into my purse and handed her 9 $100 bills.

This tough as nails woman started hyperventilating as tears projectiled out of her eyes. In a few short seconds I had completely dismantled her world. At first, she wouldn't accept the money. I insisted I wasn't taking it back and jokingly told her it was stolen. When she calmed down, she showed me a text message she had sent to her friend earlier that day that said she was praying for a miracle about her tuition.

I was delighted I could be part of Samara's miracle. As she was talking, I could see the childlike joy emanate that was still inside her, buried under pounds of pain and layers of hurt. It was her core identity, and it was childlike because it had never finished developing. Like many of us, Samara was a girl, interrupted.

We became friends and I got to know more of her story. She was raised by her mom, a second-generation Mexican woman. Her biological father was Middle Eastern, and they split when Samara was small. Her mom remarried another Hispanic man and had her brother. Samara's stepfather molested her starting around age four. Mom divorced him several years later and married a Caucasian man who adopted Samara. He was harsh, but he was the closest thing she had to a dad except for her uncles.

Samara had several uncles on her mom's side who would babysit her and her brother while Mom had to work. They were not mature men and would often smoke and drink when Samara was around. They roughhoused with her regularly and told her they were going to turn her into a little boy.

Samara remembers looking at the women in Sports Illustrated starting in the second grade. She didn't understand what she was looking at, but she wanted to fit in with her uncles and so she pretended to be impressed.

As Samara got older, her mother tried to dress her in fancy clothes, and she rebelled. She was a tomboy and Mom didn't seem to have a problem with it until she decided Samara was in puberty and needed to become a "woman." She enrolled her in charm school and tried to put bows in her hair. She frequently told Samara she was fat and smelled bad. I later found out this isn't uncommon in the Hispanic culture for mothers to be critical and shaming of their daughters.

Samara had crushes on boys in school, but they didn't seem to like her back. She equated it to being a "gordita" and never saw herself as pretty. Even though she loved playing sports with the boys, deep down she still wanted to be pretty, just not in the way her mother wanted her to be. She also found herself rebelling against mom because she was controlling, critical, and often mentally unstable. Samara equated her mother's erratic behavior with being feminine and wanted no part of it.

I asked Samara when she decided she was gay, and her story surprised me. She said it was a coworker at Wendy's who told her she was gay. She had a friend at school who was a popular cheerleader, and she would make signs for Samara when she cheered for the girls' basketball team. Samara had played basketball for years and was a star player. She liked the attention from this girl, and she would brag about it on occasion. The coworker accused her of being attracted to this girl and told Samara she was gay.

Samara said she had no idea she was gay, but that it made sense because she really liked this cheerleader. This girl was petite with delicate features and blond hair-the exact opposite of Samara. Of *course*, Samara would be taken with her, she was everything Samara was not.

In one fell swoop, Samara let an acquaintance at work choose her identity for her. She was so adamant her mother would *not* define her, she let a stranger do it, instead. This identity let her off the hook, though. She no longer had to try to be pretty and no longer had to feel the pain of not feeling like she measured up. Instead, she could "own" pretty through someone else and completely neglect her own appearance and femininity.

This didn't happen overnight. She still got dressed up and went to the prom. She ended up losing her virginity to her prom date, and said she stared at the ceiling bored the whole time. At 17, she thought that proved she was gay. I asked if she had found him at all attractive and she said no.

Shortly after, she started fixating on pretty women. When she was of age, she joined an online dating site and shortly after met wifey June. June was almost a decade older than Samara and was divorced with two small children. Shortly after they began "hanging out," June was evicted from her apartment and moved into Samara's tiny one-bedroom without even asking.

Right away, Samara felt the responsibility of taking care of June and her sons. This put her right into a masculine role and for a while, she seemed to thrive in it. She had a sense of purpose-she was a knight rescuing the princess and saving the day.

This was Samara's first "adult" relationship. She had no idea relationships were give and take, and so she gave and gave some more. As we grew closer, I asked her what the sex was like with June. She scoffed and said June was a total "pillow princess" and Samara never got her sexual needs met. As a matter of fact, Samara frequently left her clothing on during their sexual encounters. She pleased June and that made her satisfied.

Even as she recounted this story, I could tell she was conflicted. I didn't see it at the time, but several of her facets were in disagreement with each other. She had one very chivalrous facet who wanted to please and get nothing in return, but there was another facet in there that was resentful that she had to fulfill her sexual needs on her own.

What she told me next was shocking. She confessed that occasionally she met up with a male friend at an adult store because there was a room in the back where you could watch porn. She and this man would go in the room together and get each other off manually. According to her they never kissed, and she justified this behavior even though she was "married" because her sexual needs were not getting met.

At this point I knew she wasn't full-on gay. An adult lesbian woman does not meet up with a man to get her sexual needs met, especially not when they are so out in the community. Not to mention, Samara seemed to light up any time a man entered the room. She loved talking sports, hunting, fishing, politics-you name it, but she loved male attention and energy. She also loved upstaging them on occasion, however when a man she respected entered the room she turned into a giddy schoolgirl, blushing and grinning from ear to ear.

Samara had penis envy. Even though she liked her long, curly hair and occasionally wore mascara and lip gloss, she wished she had male genitalia. She confessed that when she wore a prosthetic penis with June during intercourse, she got a euphoric feeling when she convinced herself the plastic penis was hers. Her story sounded much like Kyle's, and I was fascinated at how these two people could delude themselves to this degree.

One day I broke the news to Samara. "I don't think you're a lesbian," I told her. She was speechless. I told her how I had been observing her and how she lit up whenever she was in a conversation with a man. I told her how her cheeks turn pink and how she looks 16 when a man she *actually* respects looks at her.

Samara was bewildered, and it reminded me of the day I gave her the money for school. Did I just dismantle her world again? It was like I read her mind and she felt exposed. She had no response. I wonder if she had secret thoughts of men that she hid away because they didn't coincide with her persona of being a tomboy lesbian? We lost touch soon after that, so I will never know. I did suggest to her to at least go on a date with a man she admired and see how it felt. I will never know if she did.

*It's important to note that I do not believe that everyone who considers themselves gay or queer is a trauma survivor. I do believe it's possible to be born that way. However, I do think there are times (and research shows) that many men and women who are same-sex oriented do have abuse or trauma in their past. The earlier the trauma, the more likely it is to interfere with our wiring on many levels, including sexuality. This is why facet work is critical in helping to discover who you are and how you formed. It's also key to cultivating the person you want to be and transcending the trauma through integration. When we do this, we can accept reality on its terms, and we don't have to pretend anything about our lives to feel whole. **Truth becomes paramount.**

CHAPTER

GRIEF AND LOSS

WHEN WE LOSE A LOVED ONE, ESPECIALLY BEFORE THEIR "TIME," THE results can be traumatic. I always have a special place in my heart for people who have lost a parent early in their development. It leaves such a gaping hole and as children we don't know how to heal it. Western culture is devoid of many lessons on how to process and integrate grief. Many children are shielded from funerals and are just expected to "move on" after someone they love passes.

So much of our grief in Western cultures gets swept under the rug. If you are Caucasian, you are even more devoid of healthy grieving processes. Hispanics have Day of the Dead, the Jewish culture sits shiva after someone passes, the Black culture has home-goings, and what do whites have? A funeral, and then maybe a visit to the cemetery with some blue plastic roses on Memorial Day after the barbecue.

Never has this point hit home to me more than when I watched footage of the Sandy Hook school shootings. I saw interview after interview of parents who had lost children in this tragic event, yet

I never saw a single one shed a tear. There was even a teacher interviewed by Diane Sawyer who was hiding her class during the shooting, and though she had the "cry face" she didn't shed one tear. There was one family interviewed by Anderson Cooper who said they would still go on to celebrate Christmas and the mom even smiled and laughed and said her daughter was in a better place. This was just a few days after the shooting.

Compare this to situations in which minorities lose their children and you see stark differences. Ever see footage of a Black mother who has just lost her son to a gang shooting? She is pure emotion.

Dinyal New of Oakland, California lost both of her sons to gun violence in 19 days. She cried during the CNN interview. Her neighbor, Alicia Waters, lost her son six years before, and she still cried during the interview. I can't help but compare these two situations and note the cultural differences.

I think back to my own lack of awareness when I lost my father. He had been battling cancer for eight years, and at the end he descended rather quickly. I made it to his bedside just in time to say goodbye- he died eight hours later. When I returned home, I had one day off before I needed to return to work. My partner at the time had also taken that day off, and when I told him I needed alone time to grieve he insisted that we had too much to do and accused me of being indulgent. I was peripherally aware that he probably had a great deal of baggage being triggered since his own father passed away when he was 10 years old. His mother was an alcoholic and highly unstable, and I'm sure he wasn't helped through the grief.

Connor followed me around the house that day, nagging about bills that needed to be paid and chores that needed to be done. It was evident I was not going to be able to take any alone time. If I had been thinking clearly, I would have packed a bag and gone to a hotel, but I was exhausted and didn't have the clarity on how to put my needs first.

I glanced through my planner and looked for a day I could take to myself to grieve. I honestly thought I could get the majority of it done in one day. After all, Dad and I weren't all that close and I had known about the cancer for years. I had never lost a parent and because of our history I didn't think it would affect me all that much. I was mistaken.

I was able to get through the workdays, but I was not myself. Even though I lost ten pounds, I felt heavy. I couldn't eat much of anything. I couldn't sleep. My face looked pale. I moved at a turtle's pace. I kept looking at the calendar to find a "grief" day and every weekend there was something on the books.

Mother Nature took over. One Saturday morning about five weeks after Dad passed, I woke up in the most excruciating pain. Every muscle and joint in my body was on fire. I was burning up, and my head was pounding. My chest was tight, and it was difficult to breathe. I drove myself to urgent care and discovered I had the H1N1 Swine Flu. I'll never forget the doctor's bedside manner. He was angry and literally yelled in my face. "Go home! You are VERY sick! I need you to quarantine for five days, do you hear me?"

I could tell he had empathy for me even though he was stern. I have asthma, and getting that sick is never a good thing. He put me on complete bed rest in isolation. No one was to go near me, not even Connor. He could only leave food outside the bedroom door.

This was my shiva. Even though I felt horrible, I knew it was my grieving time. I grabbed a few photos of my dad that I had nearby and put them beside me in bed. I sobbed and wailed as I remembered every good time and how I would never experience him again on this Earth. My mind would flash back to his handsome, smiling face one minute and then cut to how emaciated he looked before he took his last breath. I let all the memories bum rush me and I truly grieved. I didn't try to contain it, I just let it happen.

I should mention that the most amazing thing happened the day my father passed. He was in home hospice at his sister's house in New England and when I got there, he was unrecognizable. He was skin and bones and his hair had turned completely white. He couldn't talk but he squeezed my hand and knew I was there. As I stood there looking at him, every awful thing he had ever said or done disappeared into the ethers, and all that was left was pure love. "Death is a stripping away of all that is not you," says Eckhart Tolle. It was in that moment that I finally "met" my father for the first time. The past was irrelevant, and all that mattered was the breath he was taking at every moment. Never have I been more present.

I knew something profound had happened to me that day, and I was grateful. When it came time for grieving, I didn't have to grieve the horrible things my father had done over the years or the fact that he had abducted me from my mother. Most of it had already been burned up by the "sun," or by the light of the consciousness of that moment. A big part of what I grieved was that the most intimate moment my father and I had was on his deathbed and there would be no more intimate moments. All my life I wanted to feel close to my dad. I wanted him to see me, to spend time with me, to feel a bond. To finally have that closeness only to have him die hours later was tragic and I needed to grieve that tragedy.

The grieving didn't end after five days, but it was a start. I slowly came back to life and when I did, I made it a point to include my father into everyday life. I sometimes slept in his shirts. I put his picture up throughout my home. I played his old Beatles albums. Most importantly, I absorbed everything I loved about him. I *became* him in a sense. All of Dad's traits that I admired, I adopted. Some of them I already had. His head for business, his talent for storytelling, his outgoing nature, and his resourcefulness. I made a list of all of Dad's positive traits and the ones I didn't have I developed. That's how we truly honor the dead, and no one ever tells us. **We honor them by letting them live on within us.**

Becca's Story

I recently shared this with *Becca, a client who came to me from her primary care provider. She was 21 and her mother passed away from cancer three years ago. In this time, she had still attended college, but she had lost a great deal of weight and is just going through the motions. She couldn't eat much but when she did it was fast food or processed junk, and she couldn't bring herself to cook or care for herself well. It didn't take long for me to realize she was stuck in the grieving phase.

I asked her to tell me about her mother and her face lit up as she shared how her mother was the most wonderful person. Kind, caring, and highly nurturing. She was strong in her faith and was an amazing role model. My eyes welled up for this young woman and the tremendous loss she experienced.

Becca told me she was very excited to become a mom someday. She had a wonderful boyfriend, and they were planning to get engaged after she graduated from college. I explained to her that it was time to move through the grieving process from mourning into the "honoring" phase. I asked her to list out all her mother's positive traits and explained the process of how she gets to embody those traits and allow her mother to live on in her that way. You wouldn't believe how the look on her face turned from sadness to hopeful in half a second. She had never heard of this concept, and she was intrigued.

I explained to her that honoring is more than lighting a candle for someone, and more than even setting a place at the table for them on holidays or their birthday. It's about letting the good in them live on and continue to contribute to the world. Nature wants us to be better versions of our parents, and when we combine their positive traits with our own, we can really up the contribution to our fellow man and to this great Earth.

I saw a light flicker in Becca's eyes that I'm pretty certain hadn't been there since her mother passed. Even though I went on to create a meal plan for her, I explained the majority of our work together would be focused on transforming the grief. She was grateful.

LOSING A CHILD

This is a difficult topic for me to write about because I have never lost a child. I can try and put myself in someone else's shoes and imagine how it would feel to lose a child, but I can only guess. I have tried to do this often over the years, especially since my mother lost her own two children for over a year due to my father's choices, and I have wanted to understand her. I have had countless clients over the years who have lost children at various ages, and of course I want to understand them, too. I imagine it is a pain worse than any other and that is the consensus.

In my clinical experience, losing a child includes miscarriage and abortion. Even if a woman decides to terminate her pregnancy, it's highly possible she can carry the trauma and weight of it for a lifetime. I've had many female clients break down emotionally in my office over the trauma of abortion. Some of these women were teenagers and didn't understand the gravity of their decision until they became older or had more children. There is often tremendous grief and shame buried that slowly eats them alive. Usually, they don't tell a soul.

Conversely, some women are so afraid to feel the pain of abortion that they sometimes create a spinoff facet that becomes a vocal abortion activist. This facet believes strongly in a woman's right to choose and can get highly worked up when confronted with a pro-lifer. Their pain surfaces as aggression and they can go from stable one moment to a vicious attack dog the next. It makes sense why someone would develop a facet such as this. The grief or shame that may come along with choosing to end a pregnancy can be overwhelming, and a person still needs to function. This is a protective facet that needs to be understood.

My Story

When it came time to do my counseling internship years ago, I chose Planned Parenthood. I thought it would be a great opportunity to counsel women from all walks of life and I had been there many times myself for birth control. I liked the fact that only women worked there, and they all seemed strong and capable to me. I was excited to start.

On my first day, the director took me around the entire facility and told me I would have to learn how to work in each station. I would have to become a phlebotomist and learn how to draw blood. I'd have to go through ultrasounds with the patients, and I would have to witness an abortion.

I agreed and had no idea what I was in for. I followed one patient through her entire process. She had gotten pregnant by accident and was not ready to become a mother. Her ultrasound showed she was 10 weeks pregnant. She was in her early 20s and didn't have the extra $50 for the pain medication. I was concerned but did not ask questions.

When we went into the treatment room, she put a gown on and laid on her back, knees up. The director put a trash can at the end of the table and the doctor, a striking Indian woman, entered the room. She had been on her lunch break and was still chewing her sandwich when she entered the room. She inserted a speculum and reached for what looked like a giant syringe. She jammed the syringe into the patient with a great deal of force several times, which caused blood to come flowing out of the patient like a bright red stream into the trash can. There was a screen on top of the trash can that I later discovered was for collecting tissue and baby parts. The patient was moaning and crying, and I started to get a little woozy. When the doctor was finished, she quickly left. She had not said hello or goodbye to the patient which I thought was odd.

The director asked me to follow her into a tiny room. She was carrying the screen and informed me we needed to make sure we "got it all." I stood in disbelief and watched as she counted little body parts like she was sorting jellybeans. The fetus had black eyes and reminded me of the sea monkeys I grew as a kid, only it was larger, and distinctly human.

I went home that day in a daze. I had just watched a young woman cry in pain in a tiny room with a trash can as life was literally sucked out of her. No one offered her compassion or a kind word. She was immediately shuffled off to the "recovery room" which was in the back of the building. It was a room filled with tattered Lazy Boy recliners and heating pads. The women were allowed to rest for an hour or so before they got their Depo-Provera shot and were on their way. These women all sat together in silence. Some of them had tears streaming down their face, yet no one made a sound.

Trying to sleep that night was a disaster. Every time I closed my eyes all I could see was the blood pouring into that trash can. I heard the woman moaning, and I saw the tiny body parts. This went on for days and weeks until I told my therapist, and she performed some EMDR to help me process what I realized was my own trauma from witnessing an abortion. It never occurred to me that I could actually be traumatized until she told me I had symptoms of PTSD. The EMDR was quite helpful, and I provide a resource for it at the end of this book.

When I meet a woman who has had an abortion, I never judge her. There are countless reasons as to why a woman would choose this course of action. No matter which side of the fence you are on, I think we can all agree abortion is often traumatic for the woman. Sometimes it's also traumatic for her partner.

Antonio's Story

*Antonio was a client who initially came to me for weight loss. He was a professional musician who had finally settled down in his 40s and created a family with his wife. He wanted to lose approximately 30 pounds and when I read his bio it was obvious that he did a fair amount of comfort eating. After our first session, I created a meal plan for him. He didn't like it because he thought it had too much meat and he was trying to lean towards veganism. When I asked why, he said he felt bad eating anything with a face, even a fish. I thought this was intriguing because when I read through his bio, he mentioned a former girlfriend having two abortions. When I asked about it, he was a bit defensive and didn't want to discuss it. One comment he made was that he felt bad at the time because both times when he put his hand on his partner's stomach, he believed he could "feel life."

He agreed to try the meal plan and said he was surprised at how much energy he had. He wasn't losing weight because he wasn't able to stick to it, and still indulged in junk food, fast food, sweets, and alcohol several times per week. I suggested we look into why he was medicating with food, and we began the facets exercise. We barely got through the first exercise before he stopped his sessions. He wasn't specific as to why except to say he would be traveling for work for the entire summer. My guess is that we were getting into the deep waters, and it was too much for him. I was rather bummed that I wasn't able to help him make the connection between his guilt for eating anything with a face and that fact that he supported aborting two of his unborn children, which also had faces. Every time he saw the fish's face, he really saw his deceased children staring back at him. The irony is he didn't have a clue. When we don't process our grief and trauma, it comes out sideways and eventually will eat *us* alive.

> **Note:**
> In cases like these, it's the client's own guilt that is causing the neuroses. It's possible that Antonio acted against his own value system and never accepted it. Self-forgiveness is powerful. Even if we are pro-choice, there may be facets or parts of us who are not. When this happens, it's important to get all the facets on board for healing, grace, and integration so the client can move on.

Mariah's Story

*Mariah came to me for help with nutrition. She was 11 weeks pregnant, and her blood sugar was in the pre-diabetic range. Her TSH (thyroid stimulating hormone) was inching up meaning her thyroid was sluggish, and her cortisol was high. Her lab work didn't match her lifestyle or her body type and so I suspected trauma in her history.

When I read Mariah's bio, her lab work began to make sense. Mariah's daughter Minka was four, and Mariah was four when her mother delivered a stillborn baby brother named Dylan. She remembers being excited about getting a little brother, and crestfallen when her father told her there wouldn't be a baby brother after all.

Mariah also remembers her mother grieving and withdrawing from the family. She still took care of Mariah's basic needs, but she wasn't her old self and didn't spend as much time nurturing Mariah. Mariah learned to become independent and not be too "needy." Since Mom couldn't be fully present, they lost that precious mother-daughter bond to some degree. This was an issue since Mariah wasn't old enough to start individuating. Mom's very understandable grief left a hole in Mariah that didn't close.

Mariah had to work through some fear and grief around this new pregnancy. What if something happened to the baby? Would history repeat itself? We thought losing her brother may have been her core wound, but there was more. Once she worked through the trauma of the loss and discussed it with her parents, she felt lighter but was still having self-esteem issues. We kept going through her facets trying to determine which ones had the self-worth issues.

VERY YOUNG SELF: MARIAH AGE 4

Traits: Loves preschool and teachers, obsessed with putting things in bags, loves music, likes older kids, loves ballet, rule follower.

Triggers: Feeling not taken care of (like a burden), feeling needy and high maintenance, feeling responsible to put needs of others before her own, needing to be good and be acceptable. "If I have a, need I don't like the attention it brings."

How am I productive/useful? I'm able to care for others, I can be resourceful and meet my own needs, this part of me reminds me of my needs.

How can I be destructive? Hinders me from asking for help or accepting help, feel guilty having a need (like I'm being extra), too self-sufficient, doesn't value herself, needs approval.

What are my needs? "If I have a need I don't like the attention it brings." Wants to feel accepted.

What is my biggest fear? Being an inconvenience or a burden.

What is the false narrative? Other people's needs matter more than mine.

As we went down the rabbit hole together, I learned about Sam, Mariah's first love. She was 15 when they met and there was instant chemistry between them. He looked at her in a way that made her feel seen. What was powerful was that she wasn't trying to get his attention- he zeroed in on her, which cut through several layers of boundaries and rendered her defenseless.

Remember that hole Mariah had after Dylan died and Mom was grieving? It never closed. In one fell swoop Sam was able to fill the hole and then some with his care and attention toward Mariah. When a little girl is four years old, she idolizes her mother. When that process is interrupted, several things occur. First off, the child cannot go on to form a complete identity because they haven't individuated properly. This means there will always be a need for external approval and a deep-seated lack of self-worth. Think about how often kids at this age say, "Mom, look!" They constantly seek approval from parents, as they should. It's a normal part of development.

Even though Sam was not a great partner for Mariah, she couldn't let him go. They went back and forth for years and the pull toward him was great. He was hot and cold, and she never felt like he could fully commit to her.

When they finally lost touch, she went on to meet a great man and get married. Unfortunately, even though she was no longer in love with Sam, she couldn't get him out of her head. She always wanted him to see what she was doing in life and offer his approval. This thought would sometimes cross her mind dozens of times in a day, even though Sam had married and had a family. They weren't in communication except for a yearly Happy Birthday text message, but her brain was stuck on a Sam approval loop, until we did the work.

It was Mariah's youngest facet that was still stuck on that diving board saying, "Mom, watch this!" Only she had replaced Mom with Sam and he became the stand-in figure that needed to offer his approval because she had not yet individuated.

I was only able to present this theory to Mariah because I had experienced the same phenomena with my own first love, Edward. Being taken from my mother at such a young age (when I was still madly in love with her), I also had not fully individuated. There was still a deep urge to fuse with someone like I had been fused to my mother. When I met Ed at age 16 and he bore holes through me with his eyes, I was a goner. When I fused to him, he literally became part of my nervous system, much like Mom had been. My thoughts were consumed with him and when we went years without talking, he was like a computer program that was continuously running in the background. I didn't even realize at the time how many times in a day he would cross my mind. *I wonder if Ed would like this dress. I wonder if he would appreciate this song. I wish Ed could see this sunset…*

An on and on. A few times a year I would dig out all my old cards and letters and cry a gut-wrenching cry, much like the way I sobbed when I was taken from Mom. The loss felt the same. How is that even possible, you might ask? Unresolved trauma. It didn't matter who Edward was, only that I fused to him, and he was my literal mother replacement. It didn't help that he had fused to me, too. We both thought it was love but I can assure you now, it wasn't. If it was love neither of us would have married other people.

What's amazing is that once I recognized this deep attachment the spell was instantly broken. Edward would never have been a good partner for me, and I could finally stop making excuses and see it. In reality, he was a literal train wreck. That was the absolute end of all codependency for me. Any lingering traces of it were burned up by the light of this realization. I felt a strength and solidness come over me that I hadn't experienced, *ever*. The stark realization that the only love that really matters is the love I give myself was life-giving. Anything else I get from others is the gravy.

Luckily, Mariah had a similar experience. Once she realized her attachment to Sam was a trauma bond, she was able to break it and it lost its power over her. Then she got to discover who she really was now that she didn't need anyone else to "see" her or "approve" of her.

> **Note:**
> Mariah and her mother had a wonderful, loving relationship but it didn't matter because nothing was going to overrule that moment when Sam "chose" her and anesthetized the pain that was so deep inside her. That's why we had to go back in time and reclaim her.

THE EFFECTS OF VIOLENCE

A GREAT DEAL OF OUR TRAUMATIC EXPERIENCES STEM FROM VIOLENCE. There are many different types of violence, and they can all cause lasting scars. We experience violence in our families, in our relationships, and even in our interactions with strangers. All you have to do is turn on the television to see the rampant violence happening in our nation. Within the last few years, the number of homicides and robberies has skyrocketed. That equates to lots of trauma.

Most people don't realize yelling is a form of violence. How many of us were routinely yelled at when we were kids? It can affect our nervous systems long term and affect who we become. People who experienced a lot of yelling in their youth often go on to develop anxiety disorders and they usually don't relate the two.

Were you "whooped" with a belt? Overly spanked? Many of us got a swat or two as children, but some of our parents went over the top with corporeal punishment. Not only can this cause trauma, but it can also lead to the side effects of trauma, which are often depression and low self-worth. Many people I know who were hit as children go on to have sleep issues, bad dreams, restless legs, and substance abuse disorders. These are all indicative of a damaged nervous system.

Many people will claim they got hit "and turned out just fine." I always invite them to look again. Perhaps they're 50 pounds overweight. Maybe they're smokers, on anti-depressants, and diagnosed with ADD. But they pay their taxes and think they are "fine." Few people in this country are actually "fine," if you haven't noticed.

Remember Connor? His mother was a violent drunk. His parents divorced when he was young, and he and his sister lived with their mother. She worked during the day and as soon as she got home, she hit the bottle. Connor told me of countless times she hit him, slapped him, chased him around the house with knives and guns, and stabbed him on one occasion. The emotional violence was near constant with yelling, screaming, and insults. One story that sticks out is when his high school girlfriend insisted she come over to meet his family. Connor's mother took one look at her and said, "Your girlfriend is fat." I can't imagine the humiliation he felt in that moment.

Connor used to cry in his sleep a lot. He thrashed around and frequently dreamed of combat fighting, even though he was never in the military. He also dreamed of dragons and other scary things coming to get him. When he was awake, he was on high alert. The littlest thing could cause a meltdown. Once, when we were in an airport, he thought I forgot to pack the car keys and before I could tell him that I had them he had opened the suitcase and was frantically throwing clothes all over the terminal. He was a hair trigger.

We saw several therapists, who diagnosed him with various disorders. One swore he had Asperger's. Another was convinced he had borderline personality disorder. The sad part is no one addressed his trauma. No one bothered to ask him what his favorite painting was (Guernica by Picasso) or what his favorite song was (Behind Blue Eyes by The Who). These were red flags I missed when we were dating.

Connor was never physically violent, but he was a yeller. A yeller and a tantrum-thrower. There were even times he would clench his fists like a toddler. Every time we had an argument, he said we should end the relationship, however if I went for a drink with a friend he would text and call repeatedly, telling me he couldn't sleep without me next to him.

Our sex life was nearly non-existent. He almost never initiated, and I later found out he was addicted to masturbation. His routine was to come home in the evening after hitting the gym and to masturbate in the shower. After dinner, he watched hours of television then went to sleep. If I expressed an interest in sex, he would brush me off and say he wasn't in the mood.

Connor had an anxious-avoidant attachment style. He wouldn't allow himself to get too close to me because women were scary (it didn't help that his mother and I shared a birthday), but he also couldn't do life alone because he hadn't individuated. So, he needed me, but he hated that he needed me, and he would punish me for it. I didn't know a thing about facets at this point, which made it difficult to understand him and to empathize. When Connor was triggered, he might have been looking at me, but he saw his mother. I knew this when he would accuse me of outrageous things. "You are never there for me," or "You never do anything for me," "You've never loved me," and on. One time I overheard him telling a relative on the phone that I was just like his mother. Nothing was further from the truth, but he could only see me through the distorted lens of his trauma, and I wasn't safe for him.

Once during a fight, he asked, "What's *one* nice thing you do for me." I replied, "I iron all of your clothes." He insisted somehow that it didn't count. I was hurt and I never ironed anything for him after that day. Nothing I did was enough because of the wounds he had from Mom. We parted soon after. He was not willing to look at himself or into the dark abyss that was his past. I could no longer tolerate it.

One of the greatest examples of the consequences of emotional violence I have seen in entertainment is in the movie *Don Jon*, written by

Joseph Gordon Levitt. If you haven't seen it, I highly recommend it. The main character is a young Italian East Coast man who has a mentally and emotionally abusive father. The movie takes you through Jon's life-his compulsions, his shallow interactions with friends and family, and his porn addiction. You see how he fails to connect with his girlfriend because he has developed an avoidant attachment. He also fails to set boundaries with her because he wants her approval.

How many times have you found yourself wanting someone else's approval? Often, survivors of violence do not have a strong enough foundation and only feel worthy when everyone approves of them. The problem with this is that we will secretly resent needing their approval and become passive aggressive. This means we will continuously sabotage ourselves and our relationships because deep down we know we are selling out for cheap acceptance.

Another problem with this is that no amount of praise or acceptance will ever be enough. Picture an air mattress with a slow leak. No matter how much air you put in it, you will eventually need to put in more. When you feel good about yourself from the inside out, the opposite is true. No amount of criticism or disapproval will ever get you down because you believe in yourself.

I'm reminded of Kathryn Stockett, author of *The Help*. She received over 60 rejection letters for her manuscript over three years and didn't give up. Friends and family started giving up on her, but she never gave up on herself. She was still writing and researching in a hospital bed as she was about the give birth to her daughter. After her baby was born, she would sneak off to the local Comfort Inn to get alone time to revise and edit her book, telling her husband she was going on a girls' weekend.

Finally, her work paid off. Her 61st query was accepted and long story short she went on to sell over 10 million copies. The book was made into a movie and translated into 40 languages. The husband that stopped believing in her? She dumped him. I'm not at all surprised.

HEALING FROM ABUSE

How do we get to Kathryn's level of self-worth? You CAN get there. We must nurture those facets. We discover them, listen to them, love them, parent them, and guide them. We hold them. We honor them. We thank them. Most of all, we accept them. We make it our #1 most important job. It's ok if other things go by the wayside for a time while you are getting to know yourself. You just discovered an orphanage full of scared, angry, neglected, precious children, and they all belong to you. **Give them your all.**

NERVOUS SYSTEM RECOVERY

Are you jumpy? Do you have anxiety? Bad dreams? Are you a hair trigger like Connor? Do loud noises bother you? Do you have insomnia? You could be suffering from a damaged nervous system as a result of past trauma. Below is a technique that has helped me immensely and I bet it could help you too. What's great is that you can use it on yourself at any time and in any place. And it's FREE!

MENTAL FIELD TECHNIQUE

I learned this technique in 2005 from Dietrich Klinghardt, MD. I had just graduated with my master's in counseling, and I was eager to learn more mind/body approaches to healing. I saw Dr. Klinghardt's workshop advertised on Dr. Mercola's site and knew I needed to attend.

I ended up taking several workshops with Dr. Klinghardt because his wisdom and techniques were ahead of their time. This approach is similar to EFT (Emotional Freedom Technique) but with a few key differences. What I like about MFT is that it addresses the mind and body at the same time. This technique was developed by psychologist, Roger Callahan, Ph.D.

There are nine key tapping points.

1. Top of the head (put one hand in front of the other)
2. Eyebrows
3. Temples
4. Back of the head
5. Cheeks
6. Above lip
7. Chin (in the crease)
8. Sides (under armpits)
9. Chest

Tap each point @ 12 times in a waltz rhythm. You can tap these points with or without using an affirmation. I prefer the affirmation, however sometimes there isn't time, and you need immediate relief.

Example: Let's use an example of a fear of public speaking. Many abuse survivors can't stand speaking in public. It's often tied to low self-worth. Shy people hate having all eyes on them. Here's how we can address it:

Top of head affirmation: "Even though I am afraid to speak in public, I deeply and completely accept myself."

Eyebrows affirmation: "Even though I am nervous to speak in front of people, I deeply and completely accept myself."

Temples affirmation: "Even though I am anxious when speaking in front of others, I deeply and completely accept myself."

Back of the head: "Even though the thought of public speaking makes my heart beat faster, I deeply and completely accept myself.

Cheeks: "Even though I'm terrified to speak in front of others, I deeply and completely accept myself."

Above lip (one key word or phrase): Public speaking

Chin (repeat phrase): Public speaking

Sides: Hum in your natural voice

Chest: Keep humming

Do you see how we changed the phrases each time? This is to get the message into your subconscious in various ways while tapping on those meridian lines to calm the nervous system.

Tips for Tapping

- Don't tap too fast or too slow. Try and stick with the waltz rhythm.

- Breathe while you are tapping.

- If tapping brings emotion that's ok! Let it flow and keep going.

- Do 3-4 rounds for the best results, changing the verbiage and the key word with every round

- Use all 10 fingers while tapping

You can use this technique for nearly everything, from "Even though I'm stressed out today…" to "Even though I was abused as a child…" and anything in between. This is MAJOR step in taking back control of our nervous system and reclaiming our health and well-being. I still tap almost daily and find the results to be astounding.

Eckhart Tolle says, "In a fully-functioning person, and emotion has a very short life span." The problem is, very few of us are *fully* functioning. Unlike ducks, whom he says flap their wings vigorously to get rid of stress, we tend to do the opposite. We hold on to hurtful words and experiences. We make them part of our fabric. Think about it. When something awful happens to you how many people do you tell? Do you post it on social media? Do you get a t-shirt made?

The younger we are when trauma occurs, the more we tend to hold on. Tapping is way to flap our wings, in a sense, and release old energy from the past. It's also a great way to release frustration from the argument you had with your spouse just a moment ago. Try it and see for yourself.

A SPECIAL NOTE FOR SEVERE TRAUMA SURVIVORS

First off, if you are the victim of a horrible crime, I am truly sorry. Sexual assault, attempted murder, gang violence, being robbed, being shot, experiencing the horrendous violence from war- these are all incredibly intense experiences. Give yourself a hug for being here and enduring such hardship. You may need more than a few rounds of tapping to feel peace and experience healing. Tapping is powerful, but it's not a cure all. Luckily, there are other techniques out there. Some people go to sweat lodges. Others attend trauma recovery seminars. Getting a qualified therapist can help, especially one trained in EMDR. There is plenty out there on how EMDR works so I won't cover it here. What I will say it's a simple process involving eye movement that can help the brain and nervous system reprocess trauma. I'm a big fan.

A WORD ON NARCISSISM

I'm including narcissism in this chapter because narcissists are responsible for so much mental and emotional abuse on the planet. Nearly everyone has had a run-in with one. Typically, trauma survivors attract them like a moth to a flame.

Narcissists are experts at reading people, and they can sense a chink in your armor a mile away. If you struggle with any kind of low self-esteem or codependency, a narcissist will home in on it and will know exactly how to gain your trust to win you over. It's like they can sense what you need and provide it in a way that they feel like an angel sent from God. At least in the beginning.

Many narcissists are also trauma survivors; however, their facet development went off the rails. We have seen the story over and over in superhero movies-the bad guy who was bullied in childhood turns into the evil nemesis to the good guy. That's narcissism in a nutshell. Something terrible happened during their development and there is little anyone can do to get that train back on track.

Some say there are different subtypes of narcissism and I tend to agree. The overt and malignant narcissists are ones I try to stay far away from, both personally and professionally. Covert narcissists are harder to detect because they put on a show, though they can still inflict abuse that can be damaging. What stinks about that is that they often come across as "good guys," so the abuse is not so obvious to the public.

All narcissists are expert liars. It's truly second nature for them. My guess is that many would be able to pass lie detector tests, since they convince themselves of their own lies **as they are telling them**. This is one of their biggest "evil" superpowers. They lie without blinking. They will yell and scream and call you crazy for questioning them when you were right all along. Then they will start pointing out all your flaws and somehow the conversation gets turned back on you. When you present concrete evidence of their lies, they still don't take ownership. They somehow make it your fault. This is abuse. It's also crazymaking. If you have had to endure narcissists in your life, give yourself a medal. If you have had a child with one, I hope you win the lottery. The road with a narcissist is never smooth, and just when things are calm, they will throw something at you from left field, so you don't get too comfortable.

Narcissists LOVE to keep your nervous system activated. That's how they control you. Whether they are love bombing you or cursing your existence, one thing is for sure: they get your blood going. Trauma survivors gravitate toward this because we often lead a somewhat numb existence. Trauma NUMBS. For some of us, it often takes a lot to get our nervous system in gear and sometimes we will even take the arguments and drama because feeling something awful is better than feeling nothing at all. At least when we are feeling we know we are alive.

If you are recovering from a relationship with a narcissist, know this: they didn't love you. Did you get that? **THEY NEVER LOVED YOU**. They can't (not even the coverts). Deep down they have such a loathing for themselves, they cannot possibly love another person. This is not a reason to feel sorry for them, it's just the truth. If you are stuck on a narcissist, it means you have unresolved pain with either a parent or a sibling (rarely a grandparent or aunt/uncle). Somehow their "love" became a stand-in for the love you didn't get as a child. This is true nearly 100% of the time.

It's important to note there are just as many female narcissists as there are males. It's tough to notice the females because they often put on the sweet, syrupy act for the public. They will bust your balls behind closed doors, however, and constantly keep the crazy alive. There are just as many men out there abused by female narcissists, and when I work with them, I help them connect the dots with their facets and which ones gravitated toward the diseased partner. Often at that point the bubble bursts, the spell is broken, and they can start reclaiming themselves. It's never pretty.

One thing to note is the similarity sometimes between codependency and narcissism. When people are in the "dependent" role of codependency, they are so insecure they think everything is about them. You're having a bad day? It must be something they are doing wrong.

You're quiet? You must be mad at them. You didn't compliment their cooking? They must have screwed up dinner. These interactions can be exhausting and do tend to mimic narcissism in a way that the other person can't get out of their own thoughts for two seconds and actually *see* you. Often, counseling and trauma recovery work does wonders for these people, however they must be willing to dig deep and face harsh truths. Otherwise, you are wasting your time.

CHAPTER

CULTURE CAN KILL

CULTURAL TRAUMA IS ALMOST NEVER TALKED ABOUT, BUT THERE WAS no way I was leaving it out. In a climate where everything we say about race, ethnicity, and culture can easily be misconstrued as hatred, I hope you read this chapter with a clear mind and an open heart.

Culture creates trauma. There are innumerable ways in how this is true, but we all know it's the truth. Most people think of ethnicity when it comes to culture, but it extends far beyond those boundaries. The art world has a culture. The fashion world has a culture. Poverty has a culture. Los Angeles has a culture. The "South" has a culture. The "North" has a culture. The "Midwest" has its own culture. Your workplace has a culture. Your family has its own culture. Your college has a culture. All the organizations you belong to have a culture. Even my Zumba class at the YMCA has a distinct culture.

We all want to belong. We want to belong to our own families, our own tribes, our own schools, clubs, churches, and organizations. We want to belong in our neighborhoods. We want to feel worthy, and these influences have a lot of control over how we think, feel, and behave.

When we are young, they have dominion over us. They shape how we see the world. They indoctrinate us with false narratives to keep us part of the "tribe." They imbue us with herd mentality. If we leave the herd, it weakens. The herd promises safety and comradery, but little more. It doesn't want us to see what's "out there." Anyone who has watched *The Truman Show* understands this philosophy.

When I became an adult, I had to come to terms with my own cultural influences. First off, I was raised by a New York Italian- American mother. We grew up with many customs common in that culture. We ate lots of pasta, cookies, cakes, and processed meats. My mother yelled and was a hot-head, something she inherited from her own mother. She was mouthy and there was a great deal of fighting in my home. There were always threats of physical violence, which we eventually became used to because it's common for many Italians to threaten harm to ones they love. Things like, "I'm gonna slit your throat, break your legs, gouge your eyes out..." These were terms of endearment in a sense. My mother had her own brand of dysfunction, but it wasn't hard to see which parts she inherited from her tribe.

I also had the culture of poverty to contend with. Praying for food, having no electricity, holes in my shoes during winter. These experiences leave a mark on you. I had to wean myself off spending money at the gas station, which is something low-income people often do. Sodas, cigarettes, beef jerky, lottery tickets. I recognized early on this is part of the culture of poverty. Not paying bills on time, never having a savings account, robbing Peter to pay Paul. I eschewed all these stress-inducing behaviors and traded them for what successful people do. To do that, I had to quit smoking and break even further away from my culture (all four of my parents smoked).

My mother was perpetually unhappy in her marriages. I learned from her that all men are terrible, and that marriage can never be happy. That one took a long time to unlearn. I also learned it was never wise to rely on a man for security so I pursued my degrees with grim determination and promised myself I would never "need" a man for survival.

I'm glad I got my education, but my fear also stunted me in ways I had to overcome.

A lot of my healing work has come from unlearning things I learned throughout my development. I learned in grade school my voice didn't matter. I learned at church if I sinned, I was going to hell. My mother told me all rich people were terrible. I learned from my tribe that boys matter more than girls.

Here are some examples of cultural abuses and traumas you may be able to relate to. The obvious abuse in our country is racism towards minorities which is still a travesty that needs our attention. Below are less obvious (yet still damaging) examples of cultural abuse.

- Remember my Latina friend Samara? She told me she was raised to not like white people. She would frequently make fun of me, saying I couldn't dance, and that I couldn't handle spicy food because I was white. She brought up my whiteness a lot. When I called her out on it, she apologized. She didn't realize she was subtly bullying me based on deep-seated indoctrination. I felt uncomfortable when she focused on my skin color along with put-downs. Even though we have come a long way with racial equality, I imagined how tough it would be to be a person of color and experience that regularly. I had never experienced any of that with my other ethnic friends, so it caught me off guard.

  Interestingly, that same friend told me she wasn't a "gold-star" lesbian because she had penetrative sex with one boy. She wasn't pure. There was shame on her face when she told me this. In a community that is supposed to accept people on the fringe, she was still being judged by their standards. Why would lesbians need to class order themselves? This is a prime example of cultural abuse. I'm still a bit shocked over that one. It makes me think of Jordan Peterson's lobster hierarchy theory and how we truly will never escape it.

- I once had a Black client who was ridiculed by other family members for reading books and attending college. His family told him he was "trying to be White." They were threatened by his desire to leave the "tribe" for a better life. If he could do it, it meant they all could do it, too and the false narrative that they were doomed would crumble. He was also accused of trying to be White (and gay) because he was coming to counseling, ate healthy, and had a dog.

- A friend of mine grew up poor and raised her children to never lift a finger because it hit too close to home with all the work she had to do on the farm as a child. Consequently, her children, though gifted in many areas, did not know the meaning of hard work and struggled when things didn't come easy to them.

- I've had lots of clients over the years who were raised in strict religious homes where every move was scrutinized, and Jesus was an addiction. Five minutes couldn't pass without a mention of scripture or of God. This is abuse. It makes one feel like he is growing up in a fishbowl, and it makes it difficult to individuate and think for oneself. It's perfectly healthy to have a faith; it's not always healthy to have an obsession.

- I have heard from several Latina friends how their mothers called them names regularly for not living up to their standards. They were called fat, smelly, and told they would never find a husband.

- I've had friends who grew up in the South that were made to believe they had to look and act perfect all the time. Their homes had to be spotless, and every hair had to be in place. One of these friends was forced to do pageants as a little girl and looking perfect was ingrained from day one. As a result, she became morbidly obsessed with her appearance.

- Have you ever watched an episode of My 600lb Life? Every star of that show was raised with a food culture that was completely toxic. The message was "food is your best source of happiness" and when the overweight person tries to get healthy the family wastes not one second trying to sabotage him.

- I've had countless Jewish friends who have endured the stereotypical jokes of being cheap, having "Jew-fro," eating terrible foods, and being called "JAP."

It's NEVER ok for one culture to teach hatred toward another culture. I have heard and seen countless examples of this in my life. This is cultural abuse. Culture can teach us to hate ourselves if we are different, and to hate others who are different. It could be due to skin color, status, religion, sexual orientation or more. This kind of abuse propagates war. It also breeds depression, low self-worth, suicide, crime, addiction, and a host of other societal ills.

The US versus THEM mentality is a huge contributor to cultural abuse. We still pay the price for our ancestors and how they treated minorities during the founding of this country and beyond. England brought its "dregs" of society here to build up this land. Later, they brought slaves. In the 18th and 19th century as many immigrants came from Europe, they were also treated poorly. Even the Irish, with their fair skin, were treated like pariahs. Ever ask yourself why?

It's evident that since the dawn of man, the overarching ideology is that if one man is to prosper, it can only be off the back of another man. No matter which culture in the world you observe, they all have a hierarchy system which equates to "some people are better than others." Another great example is the whole Protestants versus Catholics war in Ireland. Look at how much destruction and death occurred because of the US versus THEM mentality.

I want you to take a moment and assess where you have been indoctrinated with an US vs THEM mentality in your life. This might take some real contemplation. What did you learn from parents? Grandparents? Teachers? Government? Religious leaders? Your fellow gays?

I once had a gay male friend who would pick apart nearly everyone's wardrobe as they passed by. One day I asked him why he did it. It was clear he was making himself feel better by reinforcing that he had better fashion sense than almost everyone on the planet. I got him to open up about being bullied in school for his fashion choices. He learned a "ME vs. THEM" mentality that he was still carrying around. It took a bit of convincing to get him to realize that no one was looking at his clothing choices and that the world wasn't against him. What was also fascinating about him is that he almost always hit on straight men. He seemed highly uninterested in other gay men and would typically refer to them as "rotten fruit." He was in desperate need of acceptance from those who hated his differences-at least some of his facets were.

> **Note:**
> I use the term Black instead of African American because several of my Black friends are Jamaican and do not consider themselves African American. Every single Black person I have asked has insisted I use the term Black. If anyone ever asked me to use the term African American of course I would oblige.

GENERATIONAL TRAUMA

Generational and ancestral trauma is often overlooked in our modern-day 'McCounseling' therapy where the model is "in and out" much like the fast-food restaurant chains. Some generational trauma is obvious-Holocaust survivors, war survivors, and others less obvious.

Murder, abuse, deaths of children or parents early on, poverty, and more permeate many families and we are clueless to their effects.

When I was in my early 20s, I used to jokingly say I would stick my head in an oven when things got stressful. One time I said it to an aunt who yelled at me and told me never to say it again. She went on to tell me that my grandmother had done that when she was younger and had to go to a sanitarium for a short spell. I had no idea! I was very close to my grandmother and was clueless that she tried to commit suicide by sticking her head into a gas oven. Even though I had no actual plans to do it, somehow, I picked up on it through the silent but ever-present collective family unconscious that each family possesses.

Another deep-seated example of generational trauma is the legacy of slavery in this country. The suffering that went on during the hundreds of years of slavery and inequality is not only passed on through stories, behaviors, and lifestyles- it's also passed on through cell tissue. We inherit trauma. Our bodies inherit trauma. It's nearly impossible to deal with something that we do not know exists. Sometimes I hear people say things like, "Black people need to get over it. Slavery was abolished ages ago. We are all equal now." It may seem like that on the surface, but the trauma of what happened to an entire race of people in this country runs so deep not many comprehend.

Here's where it gets intricate. To integrate these deep traumas, it's crucial to separate from the tribe a bit. Acknowledge the trauma and the ancestors for enduring it. But it doesn't make sense to pledge solidarity to them and unconsciously agree to endure the same suffering that they did. It's not helpful to feel guilty for living a better life than our ancestors did. Instead, we tell them their suffering was not in vain, and we ask them to bless us on our journey to get the most out of life. We forge a new path. If someone discriminates against us, we speak out. But we don't assume that everyone of a different ethnicity is standing in line to look down on us, because that is no longer the case. But make no mistake, it WAS the case not so long ago. Therefore, it makes sense to some people to hold people accountable today for what their ancestors did centuries ago. These wounds are still fresh.

When I was five years old my mother made me sit and watch Roots with her. She was a huge civil rights proponent who had many Black friends in high school in the 1960s. She wanted me to follow in her footsteps and speak out against discrimination. Her intentions were pure. Unfortunately, her approach wasn't wise. My five-year-old self internalized the atrocities of slavery and I unconsciously developed "white guilt." This was further reinforced when I was around eight and my grandfather shooed off a sweet little Black girl who wanted to play with me. I was mortified at how he treated her, and I will never forget her riding off on her pink bicycle, crying. I unconsciously took ownership of his behavior.

It wasn't until I became much older that I realized the best way I could advocate for equal rights was to feel strong in myself, not weak. When I saw an injustice, I would speak out about it. I would welcome friends from all ethnicities and all walks of life. I couldn't control my skin color, but I could control how I treated others.

Last year my husband and I were on a plane headed to Florida. I had the window seat, and my husband was in the middle seat. Directly in front of me in the middle seat was a Hispanic man watching a video on his phone. The plane hadn't taken off yet, so he was not doing anything "wrong." A woman sitting across the aisle in the aisle seat in my row started yelling at him to turn his phone off. She appeared White, with dyed-pink hair. I was surprised to see her yelling at him since his phone was not at all loud, but I decided to stay out of it. He ignored her. She continued to raise her voice, and then she said one thing that got me. "Who do you think you are?" She said it with such disgust in her voice that I had to intervene. I leaned over my husband and told her to "zip it" and that we were going to have a drama free flight. I then told the man in front of me that I thought his volume level was fine and to please continue playing his video.

Was her attack racially charged? I'll never know for sure, but it started to feel that way to me. He was sitting in the row by himself, and I think she saw him as an easy target. She was surprised as hell to find me putting her in her place and she was quiet the rest of the flight. When the plane landed, she exited quickly, and I didn't see her at the baggage claim. The passenger in front of me later thanked me profusely. He was from Cuba but had lived in the States for years. I don't think he ever had a 5'1" blond, white woman ever come to his defense before, and I was glad I stepped in. If more people spoke up when they witnessed injustice, discrimination, or bullying we would be much further along on the healing continuum.

One of the best techniques I have come across in healing generational trauma is through Family Constellation work. This is a unique yet highly effective approach where participants work out family drama, trauma, pain, and secrets in a group setting. The participant chooses people in the group to represent certain family members and puts them in the middle of the room together. Then, he sits back and watches what happens. This approach is somehow able to tap into that collective family unconscious and the results are often astounding. Check the reference section of this book for links to learn more. I have participated in this work numerous times and each time was highly satisfied with the outcome. It's best to do your facet work before embarking on these types of techniques so your Inner Superhero can show up and facilitate the most healing for you. If your unintegrated facets are still running the show, these techniques may be exceedingly painful or not as effective.

CHAPTER

TRAUMA AND THE BODY

IT WASN'T LONG AFTER I DISCOVERED THE FACETS WORK THAT I REAL-
ized the body had its own facet. Our bodies have a voice, and we rarely
listen. Many people acknowledge their "gut" instincts, but few routinely
follow them. Our minds are so loud with incessant thinking, they
drown out the body's softer voice and we don't hear it until it's screaming. That screaming can be cancer, illness, an autoimmune disease, or
a bad head cold.

To live a healthy life, we must listen more to the body facet and
sometimes, there is more than one voice. Remember Mariah? Her and
her husband had agreed that their family was complete, and he was set
to have a vasectomy. She told me she was on board with it, but there
was a nagging feeling that she didn't want it to be so final. We checked
in with her head, which was on board. We checked in with her heart,
which was also pro-vasectomy. It was her uterus that was holding out.

Mariah's uterus had a job- to grow babies. It wasn't ready to relinquish that title yet. She had to have a compassionate talk with "her"
and remind her that she has other duties (structural integrity being a

large one). She thanked her uterus for growing two healthy babies, and told her she could relax, and focus on her other tasks. I suggested she continue to give a lot of love to her uterus for doing such great work and for caring so much. In less than a few days she was able to support her husband going through his vasectomy with peace.

If you've ever studied psychoneurobiology, you would know that the body holds emotions and will often "trap" them in various parts to prevent them from doing serious damage. This is the body's wisdom; however, the downside is that the trapped emotion will slowly erode the body by interfering with the nervous system, which interferes with signals, blood flow, etc. The end result is often weakness and disease.

Jude's Story

I once had a friend named *Jude who had ongoing lower back pain. He had been to several doctors who all informed him there was nothing wrong with his back. The pain would come and go, though he noticed it more in times of stress. I convinced him to come into my office for an advanced MFT session.

First, I had him describe the pain physically. He said it felt like a dull ache, ongoing, sometimes sharp, a "nagging" pain that wouldn't go away. Then, I had him describe the pain from an emotional standpoint. He said it was frustrating, unnerving, and defeating. It definitely got in the way of living his best life.

Next, I had him tap on the MFT points with his eyes closed, focusing on the pain. He would go through a whole round of tapping and then I would have him keep his eyes closed and tell me what "thought, feeling, or memory" popped up for him. Whatever came up I wrote down. Then, keeping his eyes closed, I had him start at the top of his head again and focus on what came up in the previous round of tapping.

We usually get to the core issue within 10 rounds of tapping. The mind gives clues each round as the tapping gets deeper into the subconscious. Jude had memories of his childhood, riding his bike, his dog, and then by round 10 remembered an instance where he was five and had decided to run away. Instead of trying to talk with him his mother said, "Don't let the door hit your backside on the way out." This callousness hurt Jude deeply and since he didn't know what to do with that emotion his body put it in a logical place- his backside.

When I explained the connection, he became a bit overwhelmed. At first, he couldn't wrap his head around the fact that an emotion could cause a physical pain like that. We discussed how a trapped emotion disrupts the nervous system over time, and since it had been there so long it was becoming more of a problem. I helped him through the healing work, which was to create affirmations using his feeling words while tapping to get that energy moving. We use a different affirmation for each tapping point.

Example:

"Even though I have had a dull ache in my back for a long time, I deeply and completely accept myself." (Tapping top of head)

"Even though I have had an ongoing, nagging pain in my back, I deeply and completely accept myself." (Tapping eyebrows)

"Even though this nagging pain in my back has been unnerving, I deeply and completely accept myself. (Tapping temples)

You get the picture. When you get to the Above Lip tapping point you say one key word or phrase, which in this case I would use "back pain." Same for the Chin point.

When you get to the Sides, you hum in your natural voice. This is the only activity that takes a message to every cell in your body at once and cannot be overlooked. We also hum while tapping the Chest point.

Usually at this point the client will start to feel calm and will feel the pain dissipate or move to a different part of the body. We get a little deeper with the next round of tapping.

"Even though I often felt neglected by Mom, I deeply and completely accept myself." (Top of head)

"Even though I still feel defeated when it comes to love, I deeply and completely accept myself. (Eyebrows)

"Even though I feel frustrated when I don't feel loved, I deeply and completely accept myself AND I choose to love myself." (Temples)

See how I added a directive in there? I usually add them halfway through the second round of tapping. At this point when we get to Above Lip and Chin I would say "Self-Love" as the key phrase. On the surface this may seem like a back pain issue, but it's really a heart issue. Jude never felt loved by his mother and had recently broken up with a girlfriend whom he didn't feel invested in him enough. It's important to get this information so when your client is going through the tapping memories each round you can help connect the dots. If you are using this technique on yourself, it will be easier (most times) to connect these kinds of dots.

I gave Jude a prescription which consisted of continued tapping once a day for several weeks. He was happy to report that his back pain went away completely within a few days of our session and did not return. Later, he shared he also felt a shift in his heart space and got back together with his old girlfriend, whom he decided was a great partner after all. After his healing session he realized he was too demanding of her time and attention, no doubt trying to make up for what he didn't get from Mom.

*It's difficult to learn self-love if we didn't feel loved by both parents growing up. They are our role models and if they didn't love us then maybe we aren't lovable. This could be why Jude smoked cigarettes, sometimes drank too much, dropped out of college several times, and job hopped. He wanted his girlfriend to invest in him, yet he wasn't investing in himself. This is a recurring theme I see with unresolved trauma.

I can't tell you how many hundreds of people I have been able to help with this technique thanks to Dr. Dietrich Klinghardt. To even realize that physical pain and illness often have an emotional root cause is life-changing, but to have a technique to help release that energy from the body is a tremendous gift.

Carolyn Myss, PhD, has a fantastic lecture on Energy Anatomy that has helped me understand this phenomenon. She says if you have $100 of energy to spend in a day and you spend more than that, then you are robbing from your cell tissue to cover the extra expense. That simple analogy hit home for me. Many trauma survivors are over-givers, and we give at our own expense. How many of us are great at saying no? How many of us are diligent about recharging our own batteries? Exactly. Add to that any trapped trauma that's still in the mind and body (often held by our facets) and we continuously lose energy, like that air mattress in the basement that has a slow leak. If we don't heal the holes, we will be flattened just like that mattress. The body pays the price.

Emily's Story

I had a client one time who came to me because she had sharp shooting pains in the back of her heels. *Emily had been to the doctor numerous times, and no one could find anything wrong with her feet. No bone spurs, no Achilles tendonitis, no plantar fasciitis. Everyone was at a loss.

She had heard about me from a friend and wanted to see if she could get to the root cause of her pain. Neither of us was prepared for what we discovered.

When we went through Emily's tapping, we discovered she was terribly sad and heartbroken that she had never had children. She was in her early 50s and just never found anyone to settle down with. I don't know all the reasons she didn't find a mate, but not having children was devastating to her and she wasn't even aware of it. When it came out, she sobbed uncontrollably for a very long time. I was a bit afraid of her dissociating, but I wanted her to feel the pain so she could transmute it. Not only was she mentally sad, but her body was in mourning. Her heart and uterus were wrecked that they didn't have children to love.

I gave her the tapping remedy, but Emily was so out of it I don't know if she ever followed through. She left my office in a haze, and I worried about her driving (she insisted she was ok). I never heard from her again. I think she was embarrassed for breaking down like that in our first session even though I explained that it's normal and happens frequently. My guess is that Emily was a reserved and highly put together person and I think she was shocked that the tapping broke down her defenses. I hope she was able to make peace with her decision to not have children, or to look into adoption or other ways to fulfill her broken dream of being a mother.

ONGOING GRIEF

Not long ago, I woke up feeling heavy. I was tired and my body felt like lead. After a massage I came home to write and noticed I felt exhausted. When I checked in with my body facet my heart was pained, and my solar plexus region felt jittery. I looked at the calendar and realized the next day was my father's birthday. He has been gone for 14 years but I still hold "grief." I have had plenty of time to process his passing and I used to think that with enough therapy and self-help that all grief dissipates. I realize now I was mistaken. I came to this conclusion after watching a Byron Katie online video about grief. She was working with a client who had lost his niece and long story short she said when we think of loved ones and have tears and emotion that it's love. And why would we want love to go away?

That made perfect sense to me. I love my father and I feel the loss of him not being here. I no longer try to avoid those feelings. I just let them come. Being a trauma survivor can numb us to so many things. As I get older, I enjoy getting feelings back and welcome even the seemingly negative ones. "Whenever there isn't a way around, there is always a way through," says Eckhart Tolle. I don't want to go around these feelings for my father. When I feel my feelings fully, I always learn something about myself, and I emerge even stronger than before.

There may be some facets who do not want to listen to the body and do not have the fortitude to feel the heavy and painful emotions. It's important to let them know they don't have to do it alone, and that your Inner Superhero is here to lead the way. Some facets are actually formed in order to hold heavy emotions, and they shouldn't have to shoulder them alone. These emotions are stuck in time and will slowly erode the body, especially because they are housed in the body as well as in the psyche of the facet. They are like termites ruining a structure from the inside out. Let's make sure we include body awareness as part of our morning ritual. This is especially important if you have any kind of addiction. Usually, addiction is the last-ditch effort of the facets to not feel pain. Some of our facets will be experts at diverting attention from the body and/or overriding the body's pains with endorphins.

I recently read a quote somewhere that said, "Pain is weakness leaving your body." While that may be true some of the time, it's certainly not the whole truth. Pain is an indicator that there IS weakness in the body. It's the tapping and other techniques that help it to leave. And yes, we want it to leave, unless we have made an identity out of it. Then, we will be too attached to the pain to let it go. That's a whole different ballgame.

SELF-INFLICTED TRAUMA

We have all heard of extreme disorders like Munchausen's or Munchausen's by Proxy, however many of us don't realize the pain and trauma we inflict on ourselves continuously. You don't have to have a Lifetime Movie psychiatric disorder to fit into this category, as many of us struggle with these types of issues. For those who do struggle with things like Munchausen's, Trichotillomania, cutting, my theory is it's usually a powerful facet taking over and committing these acts. This is why these people can seem "normal" and even hold professional jobs. It's likely many of their other facets are higher functioning and not as mentally ill.

Many of my clients present with seemingly smaller issues, like not being able to get to bed on time no matter what strategies we come up with. Many can't stick to a meal plan or exercise regimen to save their lives. I have one client who can't seem to stay away from married men, despite ongoing counseling. I had one client who was also a nutritionist and had severe psoriatic arthritis. When I suggested she eliminate gluten and dairy she said she would never live without bread even though she knew it was contributing to her painful disease.

Another time I had a physician ask me to consult with a patient of his who had extreme eczema all over his face and in his left eye. When I suggested he lay off the nightly wine, cheese, and crackers, he flat out said no. He would rather look like a leper and risk losing his eyesight then to make some changes and improve his condition.

At this point, we have to consider the fact that the illness may be so much a part of the person's identity that their psyche may collapse (or at least several of the facets would) if it were to heal. We see this a lot with people who are more on the dependent side or who have a strong victim facet. Sometimes these people will not heal, no matter how much we want them to. If you are reading this book, chances are that's not you. Many of us would do anything it takes to heal and feel integrated. We want to break the curse and live our best lives for ourselves and our families. We want our bodies healthy and want to go into our 60s, 70s, and even 80s feeling good and disease-free. Personally, I would like to keep playing tennis in my 80s and even 90s. Why not? I recently watched a video of 68-year-old Christie Brinkley diving off a yacht somewhere in the Greek isles. She looked 35 at best and was crazy fit. She is someone who has figured out how to listen to her body's facet and honor it. However, we don't all have to be Christie Brinkley to live life without constant trips to the doctor's office. We just have to be willing to embrace our facets and take dominion over them. We have to be willing to take *full* responsibility for where we are at in life, no matter what our story is or who hurt us. We must give our bodies the love and support they need.

SELF-SABOTAGE

This is an important topic amongst trauma survivors and is a phenomenon I see with clients regularly. A cringeworthy example of self-sabotage was just broadcast all over the world during the 2022 Academy Awards show. Everyone knows by now how Will Smith assaulted comedian Chris Rock because he made a joke about Will's wife Jada's bald head. When you take a step back and look at this event, you can see the self-sabotage from a mile away. This was Will's big night- his first Academy Award nomination. He has worked hard at his career for decades, touting himself as the "good guy," with a wholesome image. At his final hour, he wrecked it all in about the span of 15 seconds.

We can make excuses for him all day long. We can say he was under pressure because his wife was unfaithful. We can say he was under stress for being nominated for an award. At the end of the day, Will ruined his own big moment. Put yourself in his shoes. You're waiting for the award of a lifetime after being in the "biz" for over 30 years. Would you pull a stunt like that?

I don't know much about Will Smith, but I do know he's a self-admitted trauma survivor. He watched his father physically abuse his mother as he stood by, helpless. There's no doubt in my mind that a spinoff facet would develop in such a moment. Perhaps it would be one that held the anger and rage. Those facets will often emerge at the most inopportune moments. Maybe they want to be seen and heard. Maybe they snap. One thing is for sure-there's no way that was the first time Will has "lost it."

Acts of self-sabotage are real cries for help. This is often why serial killers get sloppy and leave obvious evidence at crime scenes. It's possible the other facets want the murderous facet to get caught and stop the madness. Sometimes the facet himself is tired of carrying the rage and wants to be stopped. Whatever the case, self-sabotage can be large or small. I invite you to look at how it shows up in your life. Do you twist an ankle every time you start a new workout regimen? Do you routinely show up late for work? Do you binge watch Netflix when you promised yourself you would do something more productive? Do you catch yourself looking at porn when you promised your spouse you would stop? Do you start a new meal plan only to derail it in the first few days?

EXERCISE

List out all the ways you sabotage yourself in everyday life. Include the big ones and the little ones. Go back in time and list all of the past self-sabotage events as well. Then, see if you can figure out which facets are responsible for each act of self-sabotage. I often find the developmental facets can show up big time here, especially when it comes to wellness or any kind of adulting.

How I currently self-sabotage:

_____

_____

_____

Which facet(s) are responsible:

_____

_____

_____

Ways I have self-sabotaged in the past:

_____

_____

_____

What are my self-sabotage patterns/themes?

_____

_____

_____

*If you need more room for this exercise, please use your journal.

HEALING FROM SELF-SABOTAGE

The best way to heal from self-sabotage is to get to know all your facets and make sure they feel seen and heard. These behaviors are juvenile, and they let you know that it's an undercooked part of you doing the sabotaging. Often, when we give these parts of us time and attention, they are much easier to parent. When we tell our facets "no" to something like a donut, we must replace that food with something reasonable. It can't be carrot sticks. I suggest clients substitute with things like dark chocolate chips mixed with cashews, or unsweetened chocolate almond milk with a few drops of stevia. The Sambazon organic açai sorbet treats wrapped in dark chocolate are a much better option than donuts. The key is to take charge of the situation and negotiate with your facets. Your inner Superhero will become great at this with practice.

When you are craving junk food (or to check out in general), ask yourself where you are feeling powerless. Is it work? Home life? With your kids? As soon as you can identify it do something to take some power back immediately. It might be just leaving the room. Going for a walk. Telling someone, "That doesn't work for me." Making a cup of tea. Packing a suitcase. Whatever action you take be sure it is swift. **Remind yourself that you are more powerful than the moment you are in.**

If you roll your ankle shortly after starting an exercise regimen do not stop! Even if you must sit in a chair and use arms weights at least you are doing something. I had a friend recently who came to Zumba with a leg injury and did the whole dance routine sitting in a chair. She didn't need to lose weight; she said she was doing it for her mental sanity. That's an A+ in self-care.

Another tip I find helpful is to create an "I must" list. Tony Robbins says we don't always get our "shoulds," but we almost always get our "musts." Instead of saying, "I should lose weight" we say, "I must eat healthy seven days a week." When we commit to the Must List life really changes for the better. I repeat my "I Must" list daily. It has 10 items on it, and I'm fully committed to it. I say it out loud and I emphasize the "must." I say the list with authority, because the list is my value system, and I am married to my values first and foremost.

CHAPTER

CHILDREN AND TRAUMA

WHEN CHILDREN EXPERIENCE TRAUMA EARLY ON, THE RESULTS CAN BE devastating. Many suffer in silence and the effects are easily missed until later in life. Other children are not able to hide their pain as well and exhibit behavioral problems that disrupt home and school life.

*Shane was six and a half when I entered the picture. He had been adopted at birth by a seemingly lovely couple that was infertile. He was a difficult baby who cried and didn't want to be held. He threw frequent tantrums, and as he got older, he became increasingly naughty and mischievous. By the time I came on the scene he was injuring the family pets. His parents had also adopted another son who was nearly four years younger than Shane. In his case, they had an open adoption, and his birth mother came to visit regularly. Shane's birth mother wanted nothing to do with him and this was a big source of hurt for him, especially when he saw his brother Blake's birth mom highly involved.

Shane was drawing violent and disturbing images of monsters and robots killing people. He would create intricate stories to go along with the drawings, all of which were creepy and dark. He had dark circles under his eyes and wasn't sleeping well. After our first assessment I was certain he had mild Asperger's. (The DSM-5 has since gotten rid of the Asperger's diagnosis to my dismay).

Shane was highly intelligent but had difficulty connecting to any emotions except anger. I also suspected Reactive Attachment Disorder, which can be more prevalent with children who are adopted. He had not bonded to his birth parents in the way he should have given his age. It didn't help that they were frustrated with him and tended to yell a lot, which triggered him further. He needed quite an intervention.

The first thing I ordered was a food sensitivity test for Shane. Typically, children with Asperger's or Autism tend to have multiple food sensitivities which can impact their behavior and exacerbate their symptoms. I also took him off all processed foods with artificial flavors, colors, preservatives, gluten, and dairy. I prefer the Alcat and/or Everlywell food sensitivity tests over using the FODMAPS diet because it's more personalized to the individual.

Next, I created a supplement regimen for him which included a high-quality multivitamin and mineral, a pharmaceutical grade fish oil, magnesium, and vitamin D. He also took a probiotic several times a week.

I decided to do home visits with him because I felt I could be more effective. Since Shane hadn't bonded to anyone yet it was my goal to get him to bond to me. Otherwise, I was convinced he was going to turn into a sociopath. Since he had already broken his cat's jaw, I was afraid he was a little Jeffrey Dahmer in the making.

I instructed Shane when I showed up that he was to answer the door himself, take my coat and purse, and put them in the closet. He then had to ask me about my day and offer me a glass of water. He understood I was there specifically for him, and I needed him to invest in building our relationship. I also wanted to teach him respect, which is something he didn't have for most adults.

When I showed up at his house for our 75-minute sessions, we spent the first portion talking and doing exercises geared toward building empathy. We also focused on expressing feelings and daily living activities. For the last thirty minutes or so we played.

The first video I took of Shane six weeks in, he said he was an 11 on the happiness scale of 1-10. I asked him what he was when we first met, and he specifically said 0.0. I asked what was helping the most and he said the new foods were number one, and second our talks. The voices in his head had already stopped, and his behavior had drastically improved. He also lost those dark circles and was sleeping like a champ.

Shane's biggest fear was physical injury, and he was terrified of falling on his bicycle. His fear of getting hurt was a smokescreen for his true terror-any more emotional pain. He was still bereft that his birth mother gave him away and he couldn't handle any more pain.

Within a few months I was able to gain his trust enough to get him back on that bike. I had to hold onto the back the entire time but at least he trusted me enough to do so. I was his first adult friend.

Shane could be an absolute stinker for his parents, but he was an angel for me. He reminded me of my shelter dog, Max, who would sit and stare at me with a loving gaze and obeyed every one of my commands. Much like Max, Shane became devoted to our friendship and valued our connection. When he asked how my day was, he really wanted to know the answer. He started priding himself in being a good host and even started walking me out to my car on his own, insisting on carrying my purse.

Things were going incredibly well with Shane. He was making leaps and bounds in his behavior and emotional processing. Unfortunately, his adoptive mother Shelly, was still unhappy. She would get upset if Shane didn't want to snuggle with her when she wanted to, or when he would get frustrated when Blake tried to play with his toys. She would then resort to yelling or icing him out, which would unravel much of the progress Shane was making.

I did several individual sessions with Shelly, and it was clear she grew up with a great deal of trauma. Unfortunately, she wasn't ready to dig into it. Instead, she hyper-focused on Shane's shortcomings. She was still resentful that she didn't get the sweet, happy baby she had dreamed of when she adopted him. He was never going to be exactly who she wanted him to be. It didn't help that Blake didn't have any of these attachment issues, and so he became the favorite in the house.

Normally, when I bond with a traumatized child, I eventually pass the baton on to one of the parents when the child is ready. Often, it's the mother, but sometimes it's the father if he is more emotionally and/or physically available. In this case I was at a loss. Shelly was not following my instructions and creating a trusting environment so Shane could bond, and neither was Dad. Dad worked from home and was always distracted. He also tended to yell, though not quite as much as Mom. Every time I checked in with Shane, he told me he couldn't fully trust them. On top of it all, Shelly and Doug were having marital issues, and neither could be fully present for their family.

Things took a drastic turn one day when Shelly was in my office nitpicking about Shane. I decided to call her out in a roundabout way and see what happened. It was risky, but I was desperate. I told her, "If it's really that bad, you could look at rehoming him." She stared at me in disbelief. I had thought back to my years of sales training, and how sometimes as a last-ditch effort it can be effective to use the "takeaway" method. I don't normally resort to sales tactics during my sessions, but I didn't know how else to get Shelly to see that she needed to value Shane more and focus on his positives. It felt like I needed to *sell* him to her.

She was speechless for a moment and then said sarcastically, "Why don't you take him? You two get along so well." And there it was. She was jealous of his relationship with me. I immediately told her that wasn't an option. I also reiterated that she could form that bond with him if she stopped yelling and started using some of the parenting techniques I had given her. It was too late. I called her out and now I was immediately the bad guy. I activated her shame.

What happened next is tragic. I got a text message from Doug a few days later stating that they were cancelling Shane's sessions. I'm fairly sure it was Shelly texting from Doug's phone, but I will never know. I never got to say goodbye to little Shane or go through any termination process. It still breaks my heart to think I was one more adult who abandoned him and let him down.

> **Note:**
> If Shane had been taken to a child psychiatrist, he would have been heavily medicated with harsh pharmaceuticals. No one would have thought to suggest vitamins and supplements like magnesium for calming the nervous system. Any kind of traditional psychotherapy would have taken years and most likely would have produced little fruit. I worked in community mental health long enough to see how little they do to create a true healing environment. It's maddening.

PARENTING TRAUMATIZED CHILDREN

When parenting traumatized children, it's crucial to avoid behaviors that activate their nervous systems in a negative way. Yelling, spanking, threatening, are all hostile tactics that will further traumatize your child. Their nervous systems are already damaged from their past trauma, and any threatening behavior from you will be like brushing up against a fresh wound. If your child is on the spectrum, their nervous systems are further compromised and will need kid-glove care.

I typically suggest parents refrain from phrasing commands in the negative. Instead of saying, "You can't go play until your room is clean, "it's better to say, "You may go play as soon as your room is clean." Those types of statements are less reactionary and more empowering. Affirmative statements let kids feel like they have more control, which is something traumatized children struggle with.

Traumatized children often need more structure and boundaries to feel safe. Routine and order will be some of your best strategies to get these kiddos to feel secure. You child doesn't have to be adopted to be a trauma survivor. Lots of things cause trauma in a child's life- divorce is often a biggie. Even amicable divorces can be difficult on children. Life as they know it completely changes and some kids cope better than others. It's important to be sensitive to this and at the same time reinforce the boundaries. Sometimes this is challenging when we are busy with work, other children, home, etc. but it's critical to learn skills to avoid losing your cool and adding to the problem. I've read dozens of parenting books over the years and the ones I like the best are the Love and Logic™ guides for both younger kids and teens. Their philosophy is to create secure, confident kids ready to take on the world and I'm all for it.

Parenting is an art and it's important to take the role seriously. If you are struggling to parent your children effectively an important first step is to check in with your facets. Are you parenting your children from one of your unintegrated facets? I always cringe a little when I hear a parent say, "My kid is just like me at that age." Our children often inherit our struggles because we haven't matured in certain areas-in other words, we haven't parented our facets properly and they are still stuck in time. Their needs aren't being met and they are still buying into the false narratives that keep them stuck. The *best* thing you can do for your children is to love and integrate your facets. Let your Inner Superhero parent yourself *and* your children. This way you will not pass on any dysfunctional family patterns.

I can't tell you how many times I have had a client with multiple unexplained health issues have children that are always sick. I've also had countless clients with weight problems and/or eating disorders pass those onto their kids as well.

Actress Valerie Bertinelli has had a lifelong battle with food and emotional eating. As a result, her weight has fluctuated many times over the years. I'll never forget when I saw her on the cover of People magazine in a bikini and thought, "Good for her. She finally conquered her battle." Later, she gained the weight back, in part because she hadn't lost it in a sustainable way (she used Jenny Craig). She also admitted as soon as the photo shoot was over, she was back to overeating. I must admit I was sad for her. Celebrities make it look like they are living perfect lives, when in reality it's fiction. On top of that, it seems obvious that Valerie passed on her unhealthy relationship with food to her son, Wolfgang, who is obese. The poor kid didn't stand a chance.

I read recently that Valerie has decided it no longer matters what she looks like. This may be progress, or it could be the pendulum of self-loathing swinging the other way. A wise person once told me 180 degrees of dysfunctional is still dysfunctional, just at the opposite polarity.

The unintegrated mind loves to think in black and white terms. Either I must be obsessed with my appearance, or I shouldn't care at all. Neither of these approaches are "healthy." She still struggles to love herself, as evidenced by her statement. If she was integrated, she would realize that choosing health has a lot less to do with outward appearance and more to do with being your personal best. When you really love yourself, you want the best for you. It really is that simple.

Valerie says she is "enough" and therefore implying she doesn't need to get healthy. This is a smokescreen your facets may be tempted to use to be able to keep using the coping skills that feel good in the moment yet keep you stuck. Of *course,* you are enough. That's never in question. But learning, growing, and healing are lifelong endeavors. We don't just get off the train one day and say, "I'm done." Not if we want to be the best version of ourselves on every level. Her son, Wolf, could say the same thing, "I'm enough," as he continues to eat himself into diabetes, heart disease, fatty liver, and a host of other senseless ailments he is at risk for.

Please know I am not picking on these two people. They seem like kind humans and who doesn't struggle with loving themselves? Before writing this, I watched countless interviews with them both. What I noticed was that Valerie has a youthful naiveté about her. This is the energy of her unhealed facets, which keep women stuck as princesses. When we create our Inner Superhero and bring our facets into current time, we embody more queen energy. The queen can be loving, kind, even benevolent. She can be playful, funny, and sparkly. But the one thing she isn't is naïve. The princess still buys into false narratives. The queen sees through them all. The queen knows her worth and doesn't need external validation.

It's not ok to perpetuate a false narrative, especially when you have influence over many people. This is why we need more integrated people writing books and challenging us to process our traumas and love our facets. One of the greatest acts of self-love is self-discipline. This is the work of the Inner Superhero, and this is what elevates us to queen status. When our Inner Superhero is running the show, we integrate our trauma and do not pass it onto our children.

In the press for Valerie's most recent memoir, *Enough Already*, she says she is trying to stop saying negative things about herself. She also admits to having trauma that she never dealt with. She says she doesn't have many tools in her toolbox yet, but she is trying to learn healthy coping skills. I commend her for being honest and trying to love herself. I hope she stays committed to the journey because it's not an easy one. Hopefully, she addresses the trauma that has kept her stuck for a lifetime. I would love to see her someday radiate as a queen.

Note:
Not long after I wrote this chapter, Valerie announced she was getting divorced. She went on the Today show and cried, stating that she hadn't weighed herself since finishing her memoir. She said her excess weight was "protecting" her from her sad feelings. Hoda Kotb gently challenged that statement, at which point Valerie admitted that it just "felt" like protection. These are the false narratives our facets buy into, which keep us stuck.

DO AS I SAY...

Many times, when I have parents asking for help, I notice that they want their kids to reach standards that they themselves don't maintain. For instance, keeping their rooms clean, avoiding foul language, eating vegetables, not leaving clothes in the washer, watching too much television, and so on. I could give 1,000 examples of the "do as I say not as I do" stuff I hear in my office. We must set a good example for our kids because as soon as they think we are hypocrites all respect goes out the window. When your kid doesn't respect you it's difficult to bond. Do you smoke? If so, how can you possibly tell your children to avoid smoking? It never works. **Be** the person your kid looks up to. When raising children with trauma this is even more important since they may have greater temptations to act out during adolescence. Be a beacon for them. Be living proof that there is happiness after trauma.

SPECIFIC TECHNIQUES FOR CHILDREN WITH TRAUMA

These techniques can help anyone who is struggling and are particularly effective for children. Let's teach kids how to deal with their uncomfortable feelings appropriately, versus modeling how to check out with food, television, computers, shopping, etc.

Exercise #1 The Snow Globe

This exercise is to get your child to enter your peaceful "snow globe" and be able to relax knowing you are setting the tone and they are safe.

Sit cross-legged across from your child. Hold your palms out and have them put their hands on top of your hands. Maintain eye contact for the duration of this exercise. Get relaxed and radiate out as much peace and love as you can. Smile at your child with your mouth AND your eyes. Have your child breathe with you, deep breaths in through the nose and out through the mouth. After a minute or two you can ask them if they are in your snow globe. It doesn't take long for them to get in and feel your peace.

This is a great exercise to use if your kiddo is stressed, fearful, or just having a bad day. It can even work during a meltdown. It doesn't have to last for more than a few minutes; however, you can do it as long as you need to. You will be amazed at the results.

Exercise #2 Tree Trunk

I love this exercise so much that I do it myself each morning as part of my routine. You can either sit cross-legged on the ground or sit in a chair as long as your feet are touching the ground. Have your child close her eyes and imagine she is like a tree with roots either coming out of her bum or her feet and going deep into the Earth. Have her breathe in slow and deep, and exhale through her mouth. Tell her to feel the weight of her arms, her bum on the ground (or in the chair). Have her focus internally on the head, then the chest, and the solar plexus. Notice the sensations. Does her head feel clouded? Achy? How about her chest? Is it tight? Sad? Joyful? Is her stomach fluttery? Empty? Peaceful? If there are any "trouble" spots, give her a visual to process it. These often work better for kids than affirmations, though you could use both. A good example is to picture the anxiety as a bluebird and it's flying out of her chest and far, far away. It's also helpful to see if she can connect the dots as to why her chest feels tight. Is there a test coming up at school? Is someone at school bullying her? Did she have a bad dream?

Teaching this type of body awareness is invaluable to children. It not only helps them become grounded, it also gives them tools to use to deal with uncomfortable emotions. This technique can dramatically help kids with ADD/HD, attention issues, anxiety, emotion-regulation issues, and more.

I find many kids with ADD/HD actually leave their bodies more than we realize. The technical term is called dissociation or depersonalization and is usually reserved for dramatic occurrences. I believe that people of all ages "depersonalize" on a smaller scale regularly, which can be why we have attention span issues. Doing these exercises helps kids get and stay inside their bodies and the results are dramatic. Kids will be able to focus better, read better, and you will see fewer behavioral problems.

EXERCISE #3 THE STORY OF ME

This exercise is designed to enhance children's self-awareness by creating a book about themselves. I normally get a plastic binder and have them decorate the cover with drawings or actual photos of themselves. The first page is *Me as a Baby* and has them answer a bunch of questions about personality, likes and dislikes. The page leaves room for a photo and for them to decorate it. The next page is *Me as a Toddler* where the child answers many of the same questions. Then we move on to *Me as a Kindergartner* and continue to have them fill out age-appropriate questions geared towards getting to know themselves. As they get older, I incorporate questions like, *What I'd like to get better at is...* and *What I'm really great at is...* Seeing facts and details about oneself on paper really has an impact. It's a great lesson in self-love. They get to see the preciousness of themselves up close and they also get to share it with others.

THE GENIUS OF CHILDREN

When my bonus daughter Raven was three, she invented a game for us to play. She wanted to be an egg and I was the mama bird who would lay the egg. Then she would hatch, and I would have to feed her. I thought this game was highly imaginative, and I played along. She also wanted me to change baby bird's diaper, so I pretended. While we were playing, she kept calling me "Mama" and the gravity of the game didn't hit me until after when she kept calling me Mama and never stopped.

This game was her way of bonding with me. She used the analogy of birds so we could bond as mother and child. Having me lay her as an egg was fascinating because I think she was testing me out to see if I was "mom material." It was genius that she wanted me to change her diaper since I had missed those years and diaper-changing is an intimate and vulnerable experience.

Eventually, she wanted to play Mama and Baby and I would swaddle her in a blanket and hold her, rocking and singing lullabies. I would talk baby talk to her and she would get in full baby character. I only did this while we were playing, and I never let the game go on for more than 10 minutes or so. I wanted to make sure she got the bonding time she needed with me without letting her regress in any way. Once the game was over there was no more baby talk. After a month or so I cut the game off because we had sufficiently bonded, and I would redirect her to other games where she could act her age. This experience left a mark on me and influenced how I worked with kiddos with Reactive Attachment Disorder.

Janey's Story

*Janey was six years old when her mother called me for help. Janey was adopted and still had contact with her birth mother and family. The families were friendly and Janey's mom Linda made sure they kept in touch.

Janey wasn't adopted until she was over a year old. During that first year, she was often left crying in her crib unattended. Janey's birth mother had developmental and psychological issues and wasn't equipped for caring for her daughter.

Linda noted that it was difficult to bond with Janey from the beginning. She would often stare into space and didn't seem to like to be cuddled. As she got older, she started throwing tantrums whenever Linda tried to bond. On top of that she was self-harming through excess masturbation, and it later came out she was sexually abused by her biological grandmother. Janey was also starting to hear voices she called her "ugly friends" telling her to do awful things like hurt her little brother.

Much like Shane, Janey had not fully bonded to anyone yet. I knew my first step was getting her to bond with me and then getting her to trust Linda since she was her main caregiver. I did this through lots of creative play. I became a cross between Mary Poppins and a playful teenage babysitter. Janey responded very well, and we became friends.

When I was able to gain her trust, I decided to take a risk. I told her I had a big surprise planned. I had Linda cook up a giant bowl of jello and in a separate bowl I had her empty out several jars of industrial-sized grape jelly. We got a few tarps and put them on the floor. I had her put Janey in some old clothes and bring her into the kitchen, blindfolded. Inside both bowls I had put little toys and trinkets for Janey to find.

The exercise went well. My goal was to reconnect Janey with her body since it seemed to me like she was numb from her trauma. Because of her neglect and abuse, she couldn't feel normal pleasure and excitement, as evidenced by her compulsive, rough masturbation that left her parts red and inflamed according to her mother. From my perspective, her affect was blunted, and the normal spark that most six-year-old girls have wasn't there. I wanted to help her get that spark.

Janey came alive with this exercise. First, we started with the jello. She loved how squishy it felt in her tiny hands. She enjoyed finding the little toys and trying to guess what they were. She asked if she could eat the jello and I said yes. She ended up rubbing some on her face and body and giggled like I had never heard her.

She enjoyed the jelly even more. It was gooey and sticky, and it was her favorite flavor. This time she got it in her hair and all over me as well. Not once did she try to remove the blindfold. Linda was pleasantly surprised to see this side of her little girl. For once Janey was completely uninhibited. She was playing with all of the joyful enthusiasm of a "normal" little girl her age. It was like the blindfold gave her permission to be someone else for a little while.

I was relieved this experiment went well. I was a bit concerned that it would be sensory overload and send her spiraling, but we were able to execute it in a way that she had just the right amount of pleasant sensory experience. Linda later told me she was exhausted afterward and slept for many hours that night, which was almost unheard of for her.

It wasn't long after that Janey was ready for the baby bird exercise. I had both Mom and Dad participate and the results were amazing. Janey started bonding with both parents.

Exercise #4 Baby Bird

If your child has any kind of Reactive Attachment Disorder or is adopted, this exercise can help you bond with them. It's also great in blended families if the kids are younger. If you want to go all out you can get or make bird costumes, otherwise you can wrap a blanket around you and pretend you have wings. The adult is the Mama or Daddy bird, and the children are the baby birds. Make a little nest for them out of blankets and have them sit in the middle. Get some crackers or baby carrots and put them in your mouth so you can share with your baby bird. I suggest really getting into this exercise and fly around, making bird noises. It may feel uncomfortable, but this is great therapeutic play for the children. Have them open their little beaks and take the food from your beak. When they do, say, "I love you little bird and I'll always take care of you" or something to that effect. After they eat you can also snuggle with them in the nest and even teach them how to fly if they're ready. You may have to play this game several times for it to stick, but it's a great step in the right direction- getting your kids to bond with you.

Exercise #5 The Jello Sensory Experience

This is one of my favorite exercises and I think it's just as great for adults as it is for children. So many of us as trauma survivors have a disconnect with our bodies and don't feel pleasure like we should- often because we also don't want to feel the bad stuff. This exercise can short circuit that neural programming and get your back inside your body.

If you're a trauma survivor that overeats, overdrinks, smokes, either has a sex addiction or is averse to sex, this is the exercise for you. I would have a trusted friend or partner set this up for you and see what happens. It would be good to play your favorite music in the background, if possible. Put a swimsuit on and trust the process!

For children, you can set it up much like I did for Janey. Don't worry about your child getting dirty. If they don't like sticky things, assure them it's ok and that they will take a bath later. If it's nice out, you can do this exercise outside. I would keep it intimate, to just one or two adults. This way it's easier for them to let their guard down. If they are having a hard time diving in, you can assist them and stick your finger in some jelly and playfully wipe it on their cheek or arm. This lets them know it's safe to go for it.

Exercise #6 Food Awareness

I love this exercise because it's great for all children. Whether you want to teach your child about healthy eating or want to help them stop medicating with food, this exercise is helpful on all fronts.

You will need several different colors of construction paper. You break down foods into proteins, fats, carbohydrates, fruits, and vegetables. I use brown paper for protein, yellow for fats, blue for carbs, red for fruits, and green for veggies. You will cut several rectangles out (.5"x2") and write down foods on each piece. For example, for proteins you would write out all the proteins you eat in your home. Fish, eggs, steak, turkey, chicken, shrimp, etc. Then you do the same for each food category. For example, fats could be nuts, nut butter, olives, avocado, cheese, and so on.

Then you have your child create meals. Teach him how to create a breakfast, a lunch, and a dinner. How I normally do it is to teach breakfast has a protein, a carbohydrate, a fat, and a fruit. Of course, you could do a veggie if you wanted. Lunch and dinner both have veggies along with all the other groups. This creates a mindfulness around food and self-care. If you are a family that occasionally indulges in junk food (like sweets and chips) you can create sheets for that (I'd use pink or purple paper) and add them to meals (or as snacks) sparingly.

Having your child create meals this way regularly can get them involved in meal planning and helps them be more committed to eating better. It works much better than lecturing and helps them feel more in control. If they are consistently gravitating towards unhealthy foods, you can remind them they are not following the meal plan they created. I haven't had a kid yet who didn't love this exercise.

*If you tend to eat poorly this could be a great exercise for your younger facets as well.

CHAPTER

HOW TRAUMA AFFECTS YOUR HEALTH

IF YOU ARE A TRAUMA SURVIVOR SUFFERING FROM DISEASE YOU HAVE probably been to several doctors and have not found relief. The more doctors you see, the more medications you begin taking. Soon, you often start feeling worse. This is common for most people, and especially true for trauma survivors. Traditional medicine has no idea what to do with us.

My own health eroded in stages. As a child, I had frequent colds and flus. I had terrible allergies to pollen, animals, you name it. When I started menstruating, I had debilitating cramps and heavy bleeding. By the time I was 19 I developed a serious case of rosacea and was prescribed long-term antibiotics.

A few years later I developed horrible IBS and hives all over my body. I was told it was stress and was put on high doses of antihistamines. The hives improved but my stomach issues kept getting worse. I finally realized I had a dairy sensitivity and when I eliminated it from my diet my digestion improved dramatically. I had no idea all these medications were ruining my gut flora and my immune system. Neither did my doctors.

My health took another dive when I turned 30. I was working full time, in grad school, and had a part-time Saturday job. I had moved across the country the year before and went through a big breakup. I had thrown myself into work and school to avoid dealing with the pain of loss and of starting over in a new place.

I had been to several doctors for fatigue, acne, asthma, acid reflux. One diagnosed me with a thyroid condition and prescribed more medication. I was anemic. Even though the acid reflux was bad my intuition told me not to take the medication prescribed, which was Propulsid. Later, it was taken off the market for causing heart problems and death. I'm relieved I avoided it.

I began having terrible neck pain and got a referral from a friend to her chiropractor. She didn't take insurance, but I had heard such good things I decided to set an appointment anyway. What happened next was a game-changer.

Dr. Cohen was a chiropractor, nutritionist, and a functional endocrinologist. She had been in practice for over 30 years and had dedicated her life to helping those that couldn't find relief through traditional medicine. I couldn't have found a more skilled person to help put me back together. She was an absolute Godsend.

She did a thorough exam on me, and we went over 20 pages of medical questions. She left no stone unturned. She asked about past trauma and I told her everything. I'll never forget her words after our first session. "You're really sick, but if you do everything I say I can get you feeling good and off all this medication in six months."

I was ready to feel good and there was something trustworthy about Dr. Cohen. She was a direct, no-nonsense woman. She was a New Yorker like myself, and I felt at home with her. I agreed to do everything she said and got started right away.

The first thing I had to do was keep a food log for an entire week. At this point, I thought I was eating healthy because nearly everything I ate said "natural" or "healthy" on the package. Plus, I was staying away from all dairy products which I thought put me in the top 1% of healthy people all over the world. I couldn't have been more mistaken.

After Dr. Cohen looked at my food journal, she gave me a brief lecture on what I was doing wrong and how it was affecting me. After assessing my digestion, she decided to take me off all raw foods (except berries) until my body could digest them. I was going gluten-free and removing all processed foods from my diet. She wanted me eating only whole foods.

In addition, Dr. Cohen created a supplement regimen based on the healing protocol she designed for me. Each week when I saw her, she might change the doses slightly or change the supplements altogether. She figured this out through muscle-testing, my personal reporting, and lab work. I was also getting chiropractic adjustments twice per week.

This may sound like a lot, but I was feeling so awful I would have done just about anything to get my health back. I was taking supplements 3-4 times per day. Some were liquids I had to mix together. Some were suppositories. Some were Chinese herbs that tasted so bad I would involuntarily spit them out. Dr. Cohen told me to stop being a baby and take them. She reminded me of my promise.

Between adjustments and supplements, I was spending about $400 per month, but I adjusted my budget because I believed it was worth it. I had never invested this kind of money in myself before and it actually felt good.

Within weeks I was already seeing an improvement. My energy started to soar, my face started clearing, and even my eyes looked brighter. The neck pain, which I found out was a migraine due to food sensitivity, vanished. I later discovered it was gluten that was the culprit. I was enjoying the new foods and Dr. Cohen set up many cooking classes for her patients so we could learn how to make our new foods taste good.

Dr. Cohen kept her promise, and I was off all medications in six months. I was proud of myself for never once deviating from her plan.

It was the first time I really nurtured myself to that degree and it felt amazing. It was also the first time anyone ever nurtured *me* to that degree. Dr. Cohen always gave me a hug and a kiss on the cheek before I left, and I could tell she cared about me. It was almost like having a big sister or an auntie that was there to guide or mentor me, two things I never had growing up. I had also never had that ongoing level of care, which made me feel a sense of worthiness I hadn't felt since before my abduction. It was just what I needed to be able to stick to her strict regimen and put my healing first.

Working with Dr. Cohen, I achieved a level of health and wellness I didn't even know was possible. I had so much energy! I stopped getting colds and flus and every day I woke up excited to live my best life. I was so inspired that I began taking courses in nutrition and functional health one month after I graduated with my master's in counseling. I wanted to understand the nature of trauma and how it impacts the body. I also wanted to be able to make my clients aware of how trauma affected them, and that healing was possible.

It's important to note I was also in therapy at the time and was just starting to talk about my past. It was helpful to have energy and strength to be able to do this, as it was emotional and taxing. To be honest, I'm shocked that I was able to stay so compliant before I discovered my facets. I honestly think it was because Dr. Cohen had such a strong presence, and she was able to step in and parent me until I was able to parent myself. Almost all my facets craved that type of nurturing, and I reveled in it. She was the "lamp unto my feet and the light unto my path" of healing and I was ready.

IF YOU ARE SICK

If you are struggling with minor or major illness right now, my heart goes out to you. The hardest part of trauma integration is taking full responsibility for your health. This means if you're overweight, correct it. If you have arthritis, do something besides taking a pill that can lead to cancer down the road. Are you depressed? Did you know that research is showing a relationship between antidepressants and dementia later in life?

It pains me to say that traditional medicine now often harms people in the name of healthcare. If you want real results, you are going to have to deviate from the norm and seek out a functional medicine specialist or naturopathic doctor to help heal you on the physical level. Practitioners like me, functional nutritionists with a psychotherapy background are rare but we do exist. Seek them out. Here's the kicker: if you're going to pay for services, truly invest in yourself. Don't just stick a toe in–**fully commit** to the process. Otherwise, you are not going to get the results you are looking for and you are wasting everyone's time. I can tell you first-hand, I spend hours and hours going over clients' labs, their bios, my notes, etc. I research and reach out to other professionals for difficult cases. To do all that work only to have a client tell me they are still eating Justin's peanut butter cups is maddening. I get that it's often the facets, but you only get back what you put into any process.

Justine's Story

*Justine came to me for weight loss. She wanted to lose 100 pounds and was able to lose 40 on her own before she plateaued. She was married and had a four-year-old daughter. Her and her husband both worked from home and were both successful professionally. Both were overweight and had poor eating habits.

Justine had been overweight since she was a child. Decades ago, her mother took her to see a doctor for weight loss. He put her on shakes to lose weight and she remembered how it traumatized her. Working with another practitioner (me) brought up some transference for her. I asked her to trust me.

I ran her labs and did a food sensitivity test. It's interesting to know that Justine took a rather large prescription for Claritin™ and had for almost ten years. She insisted she had horrible seasonal allergies. Interestingly, she also had major fatigue that she couldn't shake no matter what.

Her food sensitivity test showed elevated results for eggs, gluten, dairy, and corn. I removed these and soy from her meal plan and created a paleo-ish plan for her that was low in sugar and eliminated anything artificial or overly processed. We also did a liver cleanse and I put her on some supplements to support her nutrition and gut.

Her results were amazing. Not only did the weight start falling off, but I was also able to convince her to give up the allergy medication. Since she eliminated the offending foods and supported her gut, my instincts told me she would not need the allergy medication and I was right.

Several months later, she decided to try an organic corn tortilla to see if she could handle it. She noted that her ears clogged almost instantly, and her nose became stuffy. She was shocked at the response and realized what she thought was seasonal allergies was really food sensitivity all along.

After that, Justine stuck to her plan. She was able to lose the rest of the weight and felt so good she decided to have another baby. She got pregnant right away and jogged several times per week until she was over eight months along. She had no swelling and no aches and pains. She didn't gain any excess weight, and she delivered her baby at home with zero complications.

During this process, Justine processed the unhealed issues she had surrounding her parents' divorce and her dad's lack of emotional availability. She had not had an extremely traumatic life, but she was still holding on to emotions from the past that were keeping her stuck in time. She was able to parent her facets and help get their needs met in ways other than food. She took up playing the violin and started volunteering at her daughter's school. She went from being an exhausted, obese woman to living her best life in less than a year.

IMPROVE YOUR HEALTH NOW

Everyone's health issues are different, however there are some things that almost everyone can do to start improving their health that are universal. We all know we should "eat right and exercise," however that's a general term that can be interpreted in many ways.

Below I've listed out 11 things you can do to dramatically Improve your health. Baby steps are ok, but they're for babies. I challenge you to take a GIANT leap towards feeling better and living your best life.

1. Do a liver cleanse. I cannot stress this enough. Everyone can benefit, and the results are amazing. How do you know if you need a liver cleanse? Easy. Are you breathing? Our livers are extremely underappreciated. They do so much, and we treat them terribly. When your liver gets congested so many processes cannot happen correctly. You cannot burn fat properly. You are more at risk for diabetes and kidney disease. You are more apt to have a sluggish thyroid. You are more likely to have gallbladder attacks. You are more likely to retain water. Your immunity will be poor. AND ON. My favorite liver cleanse is called Mediclear Plus by Thorne. I've been using it for nearly 17 years, and it never disappoints. If you have any kind of health complications, you should consult with a doctor first. Otherwise, check the resources portion of this book to see how you can get connected with Thorne (my FAVORITE supplement company).

2. Get rid of gluten, dairy, and soy. These foods right here are the biggest offenders in the American diet. They are so genetically modified and processed that they are devoid of any real nutrition. Instead, they are just pro-inflammatory foods now. The

wheat products here in the U.S. are not the same quality as what's used in Europe, not to mention the pesticides (like gly-phosate) degrade them even further. Your best bet is to stay FAR away from them. A gluten-free soy sauce is ok on occasion, but the sodium content is so high I wouldn't even go there.

3. Stop taking cheap supplements from Walmart. The vitamins and minerals are often synthetic and poorly absorbed. Also, many can be laden with toxins like lead. Go for the reputable companies that quality test their products.

4. Get that sleep! I can't stress it enough. Poor sleep is the cause of so much disease. One bad night of sleep can lower your immune function by over 70%. That's no joke! It can also lead to weight gain, diabetes, and even cancer. *Lights Out* is one of the best books out there that addresses the need for sleep. If you have difficulty sleeping, read this book. Get a sleep mask. Turn off electronics. Take a bath before bed. Eliminate caffeine. Tell the snorer to take a hike. Do what it takes!

5. Eliminate caffeine. I know it's hard, but it's a must for optimum health, especially as we age. Caffeine dehydrates you while mak-ing you retain water at the same time. It literally dries out your organs including your skin and will make you look like a prune way before your time. It screws with your adenosine receptors, which affects sleep and can lead to anxiety. Drinking caffeine is like putting your liver in a food dehydrator and then expecting it to work properly.

6. Get rid of coffee-even the decaf! It's laden with pesticides, and it's highly acidic. Even decaf coffee is 5% caffeinated. It stains your teeth, dries your mouth out (which can cause dental car-ies), and gives you horrendous breath. The creamers we add to coffee (and sweeteners) are often full of junk like hydrogenated oils. If you're putting full cream in your coffee, you're just add-ing more inflammation. And if you're adding oils or butter to

your coffee thinking it's healthier, it's not. It's just empty calories you don't need. Your body wants real food, just ask it.

7. Get that exercise in! And walking isn't exercise unless you are power walking at four miles per hour or more if your legs are longer. We need to sweat to clean out that liver, and you won't break much of a sweat even power walking. We need that aerobic activity to sweat. We also need strength training to build up bone mass and to burn more calories. Make it a priority.

8. Do not overeat. Overeating is actually traumatizing to the body. You are not supposed to eat until you are full. You are supposed to eat until you are 80% full. You are supposed to leave 20% of your stomach empty at each meal so your gastric juices can come in and digest your food. Many people get heartburn and indigestion simply from eating too much food. Besides the fact that your body cannot process too many calories at once, you are sending your body into crisis mode every time you overeat.

9. Cut down on the sugar. If you are a sugar addict you will need to detox. It typically takes three or so days to do this. When you do, foods like raspberries and even tomatoes will taste sweet because you are not overconsuming sugar. Even too much pineapple and cantaloupe can be detrimental. Save those fruits as occasional treats. Start eating berries each day to satisfy the sweet cravings.

10. Buy organic. All this talk about how organic food really isn't any better is just fake news. For one thing, organic food is not GMO. In order to achieve great health, we cannot eat a steady dose of GMO foods. On top of that, nonorganic foods are riddled with pesticides and preservatives. Those accumulate in your liver and are actually called "obesogens" because they prevent you from losing weight. Also, you cannot do a proper detox if you are eating pesticides. So, stick to organic fruits and vegetables as much as humanly possible.

11. Rework your budget to be able to afford a healthier lifestyle. This may mean giving other things up like every cable channel, eating out, weekly manicures, or other expensive indulgences. My husband sometimes balks at the grocery bill, but when I remind him he pays $200 a month for cable television he gets the picture. Investing in your health is an expense worth having. Think of all the money you'll save down the road in health (sick) care costs.

A WORD ABOUT SUPPLEMENTS

Some people think taking 20 different supplements will make up for poor food choices. I'm here to tell you they will not. That being said, even the healthiest diet will still be lacking in key nutrients due to soil depletion, among other things. Here is what I recommend to the majority of my clients:

> Thorne Mediclear Plus
> Omega with CoQ10
> Vitamin D3 with K2 liquid
> Calcium Magnesium Malate

These are the bare minimums. Luckily, the Mediclear Plus has a fairly comprehensive vitamin and mineral content, which takes the place of a multivitamin in most cases. Otherwise, I will add Basic Nutrients, which is a fantastic multivitamin.

Beyond this, I may recommend additional supplements based on reporting or lab results. For example, I may recommend Deproloft for someone with depression, I may recommend B Complex #6 for someone with added stress and fatigue (or MTHFR issues), I may recommend Ferrasorb for iron deficiency anemia, and I might suggest Thyrocsin for an underactive thyroid. These are just a few examples of additional support I may add for a client. There are many others. Combined with a great meal plan and stress management, I often see amazing results in my clients in a short amount of time. Believe it or not, I have seen diabetes and elevated liver enzymes reverse in less than one month in a highly compliant client.

Note:

The above are generalized examples. It's often best to consult with an expert, preferably in the realm of functional medicine. Unfortunately, these days you have to be careful because there are practitioners in the functional health world that will put a client on 15 or more supplements at once, which I not only find ridiculous, but I also believe it to be malpractice. *If you have health issues or are taking medications you MUST consult with a physician before adding supplements or following a wellness protocol.

CHAPTER

THE ART OF CONVALESCENCE

A BIG PART OF TRAUMA HEALING AND INTEGRATION IS RESTING. I LIKE
to call it convalescing because that's truly what it is. Therapists are often
encouraging their clients to get out and be active and while that is an
important part of living life, many don't understand how exhausting it
is to carry around trauma and do life every day.

Bridget's Story

It was a client named *Bridget that helped me understand this. She was a
married woman in her late 40s. She had five children, one of which was a
hard-core drug addict. She had been in several abusive relationships in her
life and was a single mom for a while before she remarried. She was indus-
trious but life was hard, and it was challenging to make ends meet. She came
to me for weight loss, but we discovered the unhealed trauma along the way.

One thing that stood out about Bridget was that she was tired. She
had a lot of people to take care of and it was hard to get a moment to

herself. She also had several grandchildren who lived with her for a period of time and made life extra chaotic.

One session she seemed frazzled and broke down crying in the first few minutes. I could see she was depleted and there was no way any kind of talking was going to help. I had an instinct and just went for it. I had her lie down on my couch, I dimmed the lights, put on relaxing music, and I brushed her hair. It was what she needed at that moment. Even though she had an attentive husband she was still lacking that self-nurturing piece because she couldn't find the time or resources for things like massages, pedicures, etc.

When was the last time someone brushed your hair? It's very soothing, and much more so when someone else does it. Sometimes we just have to recognize when we need to convalesce and do what we can to make it happen. I personally like foot rubs, massages, salt therapy, spa days, and more. These things are a combination between convalescing and self-care. Often, straight up convalescing is what's in order. This can be couch time, bedtime, lying in a hammock outside, curling up in a blanket with a good book, and more.

Years ago, when I was single, I used to have regular bed days. This was where I stayed in bed all day reading, watching old movies, eating, etc. I would normally do this on a Sunday every other month or so. If friends wanted to drop by, they were welcome, but they had to hang out in bed with me. Sometimes I'd have a few mimosas, other times it was tea. Foods were simple but decadent- a pricey goat cheese, olives, figs, veggies, dark chocolate almonds. I relished these days and felt recharged after them. I had no idea at the time it was a form of convalescing, I just knew I needed these times to keep up with my busy life. Even though I loved being active, I was always looking for ways to chill out.

Everyone needs downtime and ways to recharge. As trauma survivors, we often need a bit more. We are in **recovery.** Much like going through surgery or a tragic accident, we need time to recover. To heal. Trauma integration requires convalescence, much like any other injury.

No one tells us this. The truth is many trauma survivors are inclined to do the opposite; to overwork and over give to the point of exhaustion. It often takes a monumentous event like being diagnosed with cancer or a major injury in order for us to slow down.

Conversely, I have known trauma survivors who were stuck in convalescence and couldn't seem to get off the couch. My mother was a good example of this. Because she hadn't dealt with her trauma in the proper way, it ended up debilitating her. The truth is most people reading this book are not in that state. If you are, it's time to take small steps towards being active each day. Otherwise, the trauma will continue to immobilize you until you turn to stone.

For many of us, it takes a high degree of self-love to allow yourself to convalesce, especially if any of your facets only feel loved when they are giving or producing. It often takes working with your facets for some time before they believe they are worthy of sitting and doing absolutely nothing. We may have people in our lives who won't support your recovery time, and it is important to set your boundaries. I have known people to go to hotels for a weekend just to convalesce in peace. I highly recommend this if it's at all possible. Often, it's easier to completely relax when you're not at home looking at piles of paper or laundry that need to be dealt with.

It's especially important to convalesce when you are in deep trauma recovery work. If you are in the midst of birthing trauma memories, it will be a tremendous toll on body, mind, and spirit. Give yourself grace. Take the absolute best care of you. This may be when you want to eat sweets or pour that glass of wine. Instead, I invite you to do the opposite. Eat clean. Book that massage, plan a weekend getaway, hide out in your local bookstore. Many libraries have rooms to rent for free. Recharging versus checking out is key. Checking out is ok to do on occasion, but we can't let it become the primary mode of our down time. Otherwise, we will stay in a vicious cycle and not process and integrate our trauma. Instead, we will keep the facets burdened and keep suppressing the emotions related to our trauma.

You may know someone that no amount of convalescing or care-taking is helpful for them. These are often people who have been nearly obliterated by trauma and it's possible they will never heal from their past. This was one of the hardest things for me to accept, both personally and professionally. I have had clients and family members like this, and it can be soul-crushing to watch them continue to suffer. Sometimes you just want to shake them and say, "Wake up! You can still have a good life!" But the reality is they must want it. Sadly, there are times when their nervous systems or psyches have been too badly damaged, and they are past the point of no return.

This is challenging because often these people become a burden. They may be drug-addicted, consistently broke, full of chaos. They may have psychiatric disorders or Axis II personality disorders like Borderline Personality Disorder or Narcissistic Personality Disorder. They may feel entitled to be rescued and want you to be their savior. The movie *Four Good Days* with Glenn Close and Mila Kunis is an excellent example of this. Mila's character is a heroin addict who continuously blows up her mother's life with her constant drama and calamity. No matter what her mother did for her, she couldn't force her daughter to stop using. **We can't want something for someone more than they want it for themselves.**

CHAPTER

INTEGRATING TRAUMA

INTEGRATING TRAUMA IS THE MOST IMPORTANT WORK YOU WILL DO IN this life. It is the foundation for a peaceful, joyful existence. It is the holy grail for living each day as your best and brightest self. This is not to be taken lightly. Don't read this book and then let it sit on your nightstand for a year. DO the assignments in this book. Figure out who your facets are-not tomorrow, not next week. DO IT NOW. It's the best gift you can give yourself, your family, your community, and the planet.

The BEST thing you can do for your children is to be a cycle breaker. Let's break the curse of trauma so we don't pass it on to those we love the most. Let's not let our suffering or the suffering of our ancestors be in vain. Eckhart Tolle says, "Suffering is necessary until we realize it is unnecessary." Let's decide that suffering is no longer necessary to perpetuate. We no longer need to stay frozen in time, reliving our traumas to varying degrees. We don't need the program of trauma running in the background of our lives anymore, taking up precious RAM. We will take the lesson and we will move on lighter and freer and most of all, **stronger.**

On the next page you will find my top 20 rules for integrating trauma to live your best life. If you do these things, you will break out of the cage you have been living in. Our cages are almost always self-imposed, but we no longer need the false security of those bars. Time to get started.

Join me on this journey.

Welcome to your Uncaged life!

THE 21 BEST WAYS
TO INTEGRATE TRAUMA

01 Do ALL of the exercises in this book and get to know your facets REALLY well. Check in with them daily.

02 Go to bed at a reasonable time. Get 8 hours of sleep. If you don't, you will be too tired and too full of brain fog to make this a priority.

03 *Really* work with your facets and parent them to give up hard and soft addictions. If you are on social media too much, give yourself a time limit. If you spend too much money, put yourself (and your facets) on an allowance.

04 Do you have a drug or alcohol problem? Get help! Otherwise, you're just pushing the pause button on healing. There IS help out there if you really want it.

05 Find a friend to do the facet work with. It enriches the experience and helps keep you accountable.

06 Make a list of all the things you (and your facets) enjoy and fit 1-2 of them into your daily schedule. Even if it's a cup of tea and a walk around the block, that's a good start.

07 Make a list of 50 things you like/love/appreciate about yourself. Spend time on it. When you get to 50 go to 100. Put this list somewhere you will see it regularly. Remind yourself of how precious you are.

08 Hang a picture of your younger self where you can look at it daily. Remind yourself that you are still that precious person, and you still need to take care of him/her.

09 Do the MFT tapping as often as you can. I still try and do it daily. It really gets that trauma energy moving and works wonders for your nervous system and reprogramming faulty thinking.

10 Believe in something greater than yourself. Over the course of my career, the most depressed and hopeless people I have worked with were almost always people without some kind of faith or spiritual connection.

11 Stop letting your facets make your food choices. Start eating like an adult and make good food choices. Trauma survivors are more prone to disease, and we need to combat that with high-quality foods.

12 Get some exercise regularly. Walking is good but you need more. Combining exercise with a hobby is even better. Tennis, dancing, roller skating-these will do wonders for mind AND body and will most likely make some of your facets quite happy.

13 If you're in a toxic relationship, set your boundaries. If your partner cannot honor your boundaries, consider moving on. If your partner is abusive, get help immediately. Leaving may take time and planning and that's ok.

14 Find a GOOD therapist. Lots of therapists today advertise that they work with trauma but very few have had real training. Ask around. Have a conversation with a therapist before booking an appointment. You may have to interview several before you find what you're looking for. Ask what techniques they use to help heal and integrate trauma. If they don't have any move on.

15 Set boundaries with people in your life who drain your energy. Learn how to really say NO. My favorite way of saying no is, "That doesn't work for me." It's an inarguable statement. I also like, "This conversation is making me uncomfortable." It's time to really speak up for yourself, and your Inner Superhero facet will lead the way. Let's not eat another sh*t sandwich from friends, family, loved ones, or even that annoying coworker.

16 If you're a parent, let's also set boundaries with the kids. Kids are a blessing but can drain us with constant pestering and whining. It's ok to tell your children NO and to let them know you need space away from them from time to time. Consequences for poor behavior are a must! This will allow you to be more calm and less triggered so you can parent as your best self.

17 If you tend to procrastinate, give it over to your Inner Superhero. Have him/her sit down and make daily "to accomplish" lists that are reasonable and doable. Go to my website and get *Uncaged, The Planner* and start filling it out daily. It will help you avoid procrastination and become more productive.

18 List out what you want to Be, Do, and Have in 1 year, 3 years and 5 years. Don't hold back! This exercise, from Brian Tracy, really changed my life.

19 Create your "I Must" list and read it daily during your morning routine. Put at least 10 things on it. When you read it out loud read it with certainty. Get a picture of someone you admire and read it looking at them. It can help with accountability.

20 At the end of the day, do a short meditation or prayer about what you are grateful for. Crawl in bed a bit early so you can relax and get tired. Instead of watching tv or being on your phone reread this book to see where you still need to grow and commit to it. Take some magnesium at least an hour before bed. Put on a sleep mask. Turn on your noise machine. And get an amazing night's sleep!

21 Follow me on Facebook, Instagram, and YouTube™ for ideas and suggestions on trauma integration and wellness tips.

RESOURCES

Below is a list of resources that I find invaluable. I highly recommend them all.

1. MFT (Mental Field Therapy) www.rogercallahan.com
2. *The Seat of the Soul* by Gary Zukav
3. *The Addict's Loop* by Rene Eram
4. *Change the Way You Heal* by Aristotle Economou
5. *Lights Out* by T.S. Wiley
6. *The Constellation Approach* by Jamy and Peter Faust
7. EMDR www.emdr.com
8. *Grounded Spirituality* by Jeff Brown
9. *The Body Keeps the Score* by Bessel Van der Kolk
10. *Facing Love Addiction* by Pia Mellody
11. *Boundaries* by Henry Cloud
12. *12 Rules for Life* by Jordan Peterson
13. Thorne Research* https://www.thorne.com/u/healthologie
14. Functional Medicine and Nutrition www.ifm.org*
15. *The Power of Now* by Eckhart Tolle**

**You will also find additional resources by going to my site
www.healthologie.com or www.sparrowspaulding.com**

*Anyone who reads this book and goes to the Thorne link above gets 15% off anything they order. That is my gift to you to help encourage you to take back your health and make yourself a priority!

**I want to make a disclaimer about The Power of Now. The first time I read it, I had barely scratched the surface of my trauma recovery work. I found this book and it felt like an absolute lifeline for me. For years I embodied its principles and felt a sense of peace I had never known. It was an oasis on my healing journey, but I couldn't stay there. The longer I stayed there the more the trauma was pushed down. I wanted the peace The Power of Now provides, but I hadn't earned it. I hadn't waded through everything that happened to me. As a result, I slowly became numb. Instead of confronting people when they crossed my boundaries, I "took the high road." I "let it go" and meditated it away. I chose a false sense of peace over truth and authenticity, but I thought that was what I was supposed to do.

It wasn't until a very painful divorce caused me to really look inside and realize I still had so much hurt, anger, and pure trauma from my past that no amount of "living in the now" was going to take away. Eckhart doesn't address this in his book except for one passage. He says, "Whenever there isn't a way around, there is a way through." There was no way I was getting around what happened to me. I had to go *through* it and truly integrate it.

Now that I have done that and continue to do it, I can use the techniques in The Power of Now from my authentic self. They are tools my Inner Superhero can use when she feels necessary. We must remember that feeling is human and is very much a part of life. I don't want to meditate myself to a place of not feeling or not caring what's going on around me because "it is what it is." Some things are appropriate to let go of, and some are worthy of addressing. It's up to me and my inner team to decide.

I don't recommend reading this book until you have really gotten to know your facets and have integrated a great deal of your trauma.

Remember how I said in the beginning I felt like I started my healing journey in the middle? I want you to be able to start at the beginning. Take your time and don't rush it. Uncover every stone. They are your stones, and they are worthy of your attention. This is the most important work you will do in life.

Hug yourself from me and blessings on your journey!

 Sparrow

CPSIA information can be obtained
at www.ICGtesting.com
Printed in the USA
BVHW062001061122
651208BV00001B/5